KU-306-535

The GUINNESS Book of
Woodland Birds

Britain's Natural Heritage

The GUINNESS Book of
WOODLAND
BIRDS

Michael Everett

Illustrations by R A Hume

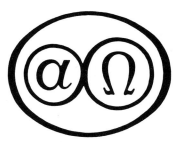

GUINNESS SUPERLATIVES LIMITED
2 CECIL COURT, LONDON ROAD, ENFIELD, MIDDLESEX

© Guideway Publishing Ltd 1980
Produced by Guideway Publishing Ltd
Published in 1980 by Guinness Superlatives Ltd,
2 Cecil Court, London Road, Enfield, Middlesex EN2 6DJ

Guinness is a registered trademark of
Guinness Superlatives Ltd

All rights reserved. No part of this publication may be
reproduced in any form or by any means without the prior
permission of Guinness Superlatives Ltd.

Everett, Michael
The Guinness book of woodland birds.
- (Britain's natural heritage).
1. Forest birds - Great Britain
1. Title II. Book of woodland birds III. Series
598.2'941   QL690.G7

ISBN 0-85112-301-5

Printed by Morrison & Gibb Ltd, Edinburgh

The Publishers are grateful to the Nature Conservancy Council for
permission to reproduce the list of National Nature Reserves.

The Publishers wish to thank the following for their permission
to reproduce photographs:
Front cover: (Pair of Jays at nest) Dennis Green
J.A. Baily (Ardea Photographics):111. Frank
Blackburn:51,53,65,67,69,71,73,75,77,81,83,87,91,93,95,9-
7,99,101,107,109,113,117,119,121,129,131,133,137,139,141,
145,149. Andre Fatras (Ardea Photographics):127. Dennis
Green (Bruce Coleman Ltd):59,105,115.143. Udo Hirsch (Bruce
Coleman Ltd): 135. Derek Middleton (Bruce Coleman): 85,89,
S.C. Porter (Bruce Coleman Ltd): 103 Hans Reinhard (Bruce
Coleman Ltd): 55,56,61,63,79,123,147.R.S.P.B: 125.

Introduction

Writing a book on the birds of woodland is a somewhat daunting task: the nature of the habitat is often so complex and variable, and the amount of information available on its birds so vast (especially that which has been gathered in the last 25 years) that producing a simple guide is exceedingly difficult. But what I have sought to do here is to write what is in effect an introduction to the subject, with the beginner or non-expert very much in mind, giving a brief but hopefully accurate summary of the history and nature of our woodland birds. Because I am aiming at the beginner, I have also included a section on birdwatching generally, slanted strongly towards birdwatching in woodland, and because the subjects of this book are very much tied up with the future of woodland I have also included a section on conservation.

This is not, therefore, a comprehensive work either on woodlands as such or on woodland birds; nor is it intended to be a complete identification guide to the birds found in woodlands. It is a 'primer' which, I hope, will stimulate the reader to move on to more detailed works which exist on these subjects. Several of these are given in the chapter on birdwatching, and include some on which I relied for background information, particularly Eric Simms' book and *The Nature Conservation Review*.

Contents

The Diversity of the British Isles

Before we look at the story of how our woodland developed, and examine its actual nature, it is necessary to consider the nature of the British Isles themselves and the various main factors which give rise to the diversity of landscape and habitats we know today: geographical position; the nature of our climate—and the variations in this; and the geology which gives rise to the various soil types which, in their turn, exert a considerable influence over the type of woodland present. The picture is a complex one, but we can at least sketch in the broad outline.

The geographical position of the British Isles is important in itself in terms of the effect it has on the type of climate we experience. These islands lie on the outer edge of the European land mass and, importantly, are isolated from it and surrounded by seas. They fall within the northern temperate zone, as does the nearest part of continental Europe, but unlike the greater part of the Continent itself they are strongly influenced by what is known as an 'oceanic climate'. An oceanic climate favours mainly broadleaved woodland as the climax type of vegetation, but there are important regional differences brought about by variations in climate, physiography and geology,

Rainfall

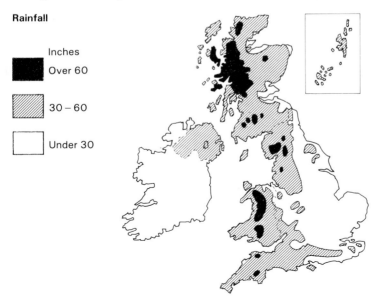

Inches

■ Over 60

▨ 30 – 60

□ Under 30

which in their turn result in the development of a range of different soil types and, ultimately, in the use of the landscape by man.

Broadly speaking, there is an excess of rainfall over evaporation, most marked in the north and the west. Where this is most marked it leads to a considerable loss of soil nutrients by the process of leaching out, which results in waterlogged soils and the formation of deposits of peat—all of which means an important inhibition of tree growth. Overlying this, there is also a gradual decrease in average temperatures as one moves northwards and, of equal importance, an increase in the 'oceanic' influence as one moves westwards, away from the sheltered eastern side of the islands where they face the main continental land mass, and towards the open seas to the west: this second factor means a gradual decrease in the overall range of temperatures, more rainfall, greater general humidity and more and stronger winds.

Already one can see complications in defining the main zones of climatic influence and working out what these might mean in terms of plant growth and, for our purposes, the development of woodland. But there is still another complication, this time a purely physical one, and this is the distribution of high ground. Most of our uplands lie in the north and west. Greater altitude in itself leads to a higher level of rainfall, more humidity, more cloud and more wind, as well as to a gradual decrease in temperature as one goes higher. In their turn, all

Land over 800 ft
(shown approximately)

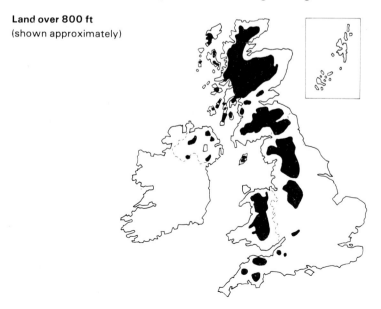

these things tend to increase the tendency towards oceanic conditions as we progress westwards—but it is important to realise that, because the general south-to-north gradient in temperatures applies, the oceanic conditions found in south-west England and western Wales are noticeably warmer than those of north-west Scotland and the northern isles. Thus, we can see that there is an oceanic influence of some sort over a considerable part of the British Isles; the closest we get to 'Continental' conditions is in the eastern part of the country, away from the influence of the sea, from inland East Anglia north to parts of the eastern Highlands in Scotland. The nearest we get to a 'Mediterranean' type of climate—not to be taken too literally, but really meaning the sort of climatic conditions which apply over the southern part of mainland Europe—is in the extreme south-west of England.

In terms of the general conditions available for plant growth, there is a gradual increase in climatic and purely physical severity if one draws an imaginary line from, say, south-east England to north-west Scotland; towards the north-western end of this gradient, we also find that there is a change in the 'altitude factor'—the limits of tree growth, or the 'tree-line', occur at a much lower altitude in the far north-west than further south.

In spite of the fact that the occurrence of rich calcareous rocks (e.g., chalk and limestone in the south and east, and carboniferous and other limestones in the north and west) is rather erratic, the richness of their soils is affected quite considerably by such factors as topography and climate. This means that, although theoretically rich rocks in terms of the production of fertile soil do occur in many parts of the higher, wetter and cooler north and west among the older, harder rocks which form most of our uplands, generally speaking the northern and western parts of the British Isles contain the greatest proportion of poorer, mainly acidic soils. The basically low-lying country of the south and east lies over younger, softer rocks, which produce richer and more fertile soils in themselves, enhanced by the addition of still more nutrients from the alluvial soils laid down by the many broad, slow-flowing rivers of the lowlands.

All in all, these considerations would lead one to the conclusion that the lower-lying south and east should have the richest woodlands, or those which approximate most closely to the climax type of forest we have said should exist in our mainly oceanic climate. With some important local exceptions, this is broadly true—but it is also true that it is this very region which is likely to be exploited most heavily by agricultural man. As we shall see, this has indeed been the case.

Origins of Today's Woodlands

One very important factor has shaped the pattern of distribution of the wildlife we know in the British Isles today—glaciation. Much of what we now see around us is the result of conditions improving since the last phase of the Ice Age some 20 000 years ago—with the important rider that it has been extensively modified and even radically altered by the activities of man during the last 2000 years or so.

The fossil record is poor as far as birds are concerned, and certainly incomplete, largely because the relatively fragile bones of birds make poor fossils, but, from what information we have, we can deduce that many of the woodland birds we know today were present in these islands a million years ago. Our knowledge of the presence of tree species (and indeed other plants) is reasonably good, thanks to the remarkable capacity for preservation shown by the hard outer cases of pollen grains which have survived in the ground for many thousands of years. By recording their presence or absence in deposits of known age we can plot the history of our vegetation with a reasonable degree of confidence. Many of the species we know today were likewise present

The Great Ice Age

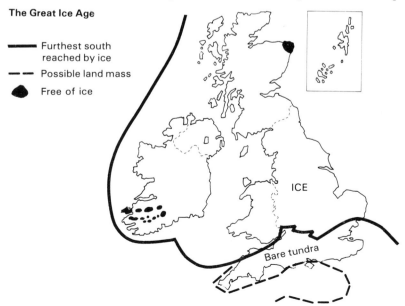

━━━ Furthest south
reached by ice

━ ━ Possible land mass

◆ Free of ice

ICE

Bare tundra

here well before the onset of the great Ice Age of the Pleistocene era.
The ice reached the southernmost limits of its spread perhaps
113 000 years ago, when it stopped at a line roughly joining the Bristol
Channel and the Thames Estuary, and also covered most of north-west
continental Europe. At best, the areas to the south of the ice would
have been truly arctic in aspect—open tundra that, in western Europe,
gradually graded into tundra with some dwarf scrub. It is unlikely that
the next stage, the grading of this tundra into what we would now call
boreal coniferous forest, or *taiga*, occurred much further north than
central Spain and northern Italy. Deciduous woodland had probably
retreated to last toeholds along the northern shores of the Mediterranean. It is uncertain whether any pockets of woodland (such as birch)
survived further north, but as far as the British Isles are concerned this
is generally considered unlikely. It is a fair guess that in these islands all
the pre-glacial plants and animals which had occurred in warmer times
were totally obliterated. Twice again the ice came south after
retreating, but it never came as far down as it had done in 'phase one'
of this last great Ice Age: in 'phase two' it covered Ireland, central
Wales and most of northern and eastern England (roughly 70 000 years
ago) and in 'phase three', following a reasonably long mild period, it
affected Scotland and Wales and parts of northern England (roughly
20 000 years ago).

Limits of the final glaciation

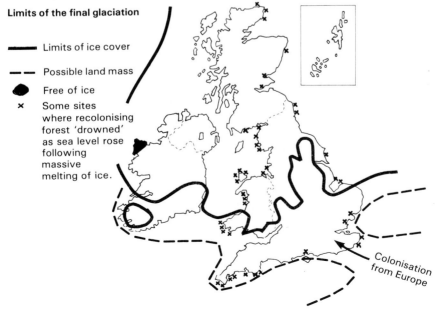

———— Limits of ice cover

— — Possible land mass

⬤ Free of ice

✗ Some sites
where recolonising
forest 'drowned'
as sea level rose
following
massive
melting of ice.

Colonisation from Europe

Even during the milder periods between these phases of glaciation, conditions here would have been more or less arctic, so that no major recolonisation by plants was possible until after the end of 'phase three'. Thereafter, as the ice gradually retreated and the climate slowly improved, a slow recolonisation by plants and animals took place, probably largely via the land-bridge that joined the British Isles to the continent of Europe until somewhere around 5000 – 6000 BC. Most of the northern and western islands were probably separated from mainland Britain long before this (in fact, this separation may date back to before the last Ice Age) and it is believed that Ireland too was detached a thousand years or more before the appearance of the English Channel.

By about 11 000 BC the change from arctic conditions to sub-artic and even temperate conditions was well under way: the open tundra was then being colonised by dwarf birch, willow and juniper, probably with woodland birds like redpolls and willow warblers among the first new colonists in this new habitat. As the birchwoods grew in size and extent, it seems likely that species such as redwings, fieldfares and bramblings moved in—species which are typical today of such conditions in northern Europe. Not far behind came the pine, bringing with it more and more woodland bird species and beginning to push out the birch and establish itself as a dominant woodland type perhaps 7000 years ago. Birds present by then probably included such typical birds of the northern pinewoods we know today as capercaillie, crested tit, crossbill and siskin—as well as several others which we connect equally with broadleaved woodland and whose origins here are rather obscure. So far, apart from the pioneering birches and willows, rather few broadleaved trees had appeared and those that had made little impact: it was not until a generally wetter and milder type of climate began to predominate (roughly 5500 BC) that alder began to spread and increase and great advances were made by oak, ash, elm and hazel, which were the main newcomers although other species, for example beech, lime, hornbeam and yew, also became dominant on a more local scale.

The limits of expansion by broadleaved woodland were set by the factors we mentioned briefly above—altitude, climate and exposure and, notably, the extent to which the soil was waterlogged. This last factor is important to bear in mind since the new, wetter climate must have increased waterlogging in the north and west to a considerable extent, probably much reducing the total area of pine and other woodland as bog-type vegetation took over on the more poorly drained areas. But, by about 2500 BC, the 'climatic optimum' reached during this mild, wet period had also brought about one very important change in the woodland make-up of the British Isles—the emergence of broadleaved woodlands as dominant habitat types over a large part of the country. Oaks were particularly prominent and other important species were elm, alder, lime, ash and hazel (which had, in fact, had its own heyday somewhat earlier in the colonising phase), plus hawthorn, blackthorn, willow, rowan, wild cherry, aspen and holly. In lowland Britain, somewhat later there was the important emergence of beech, hornbeam, field maple, poplar and others as locally dominant species.

During the whole of this great era of expansion by broadleaved woodland, probably all the woodland birds we know today became well established, although how and when they did so and in what order is largely a matter of speculation. Nor can we be sure whether some of them had arrived earlier during the period of pine colonisation and expansion and then spread into the new deciduous woodlands, or whether they actually spread into the pines after arriving with the broadleaved trees. A great many species occur in both types of woodland today—unfortunately we shall probably never know how or why this came about! What we can say, though, is that by some time during this period the basic pattern of woodland bird distribution which we can still detect today, even after some 2000 years of 'interference' by man, became firmly established. A list of bird species which might actually have arrived with the broadleaved woodland would also be speculative, but probable candidates are generally reckoned to be green and lesser spotted woodpeckers, nuthatch, great and marsh tits, nightingale, blackcap, garden warbler, wood warbler and hawfinch among the 50 species featured particularly in this book.

By about 2000 BC the climate had changed yet again, becoming noticeably drier, and for the first time a wholly new factor appeared on the scene and began to have a significant effect—man. Neolithic man with his new metal tools became both a cultivator and a grazier on the rather higher, drier chalk and limestone uplands where he began the first real clearances of the woodlands which were established there—beech, ash and yew. Later, Bronze Age man extended these clearances still further: from now on, the human factor was to be inextricably bound up with the history of woodland and its management, with important long-term effects on its birds and other wildlife, as we shall see in the next section.

One more important natural development remains to be mentioned—the onset of a generally much cooler climatic phase which began about 500 BC and which, with assorted and relatively minor fluctuations, continues to this very day. It brought with it some noticeable changes. In upland areas and in the north generally the tree-line became somewhat lower in purely altitudinal terms and there was also a slight southward shift in the boundaries of the more 'northern' life-zones which had been in retreat throughout the period of optimum climate. More importantly, more waterlogged ground, including marshland, took over in many northern areas, giving rise to the extensive system of peatbogs which are characteristic of many areas of Ireland and northern Britain today. These increased still further in the thirteenth century when a particularly cool period followed several centuries of rather milder conditions.

To bring the climatic picture fully up-to-date, mention must also be made of a generally milder but actually rather wetter period during the first half of this century. This period of general climatic amelioration led to some important northward spreads by a number of woodland birds, as mentioned in the individual species accounts in this book: birds involved in a general spread into north-west Scotland have included great spotted woodpecker (in this case actually a recolonisation), garden warbler, wood warbler, chiffchaff, tree pipit and chaffinch. Some of these expansions in range have continued into the present period of slightly cooler weather which seems to have been experienced over the whole of north-west Europe during the last 20 years or so. This new period has also brought with it the colonisation of parts of northern Scotland by an increasing number of northern European birds, among them several woodland or near-woodland species such as fieldfare, redwing and wryneck, and possibly also spotted woodpecker, while at the other end of the country some more 'southern' species have gone into decline—such as the woodlark and, intriguingly, the wryneck again. We shall return later to some of these birds in the general section on woodland birds.

Woodlands and Man

The significant but relatively small-scale clearances started by neolithic and Bronze Age men began a process of human control over the fortunes of woodland which continues to this very day: in considering our woodlands and their birds we must think very much in terms of a landscape shaped by the activities of man. Fortunately, the history of this most complex of all wildlife habitats has been particularly well documented, especially in the period since medieval times: in fact we have far more evidence on woodlands than on any other type of habitat. This is of obvious importance to naturalists of all disciplines, especially perhaps in these days of habitat management and manipulation for conservation purposes. A good deal of the evidence of what will happen following this or that kind of woodland management is already there for all to see. Equally, we should not overlook the fact that the present distribution of woodlands and the evidence of management that they contain are very valuable in purely historical terms: in a sense they are almost living monuments to times long gone, giving us many clues about the social and economic history of our islands. This point is very often overlooked by many naturalists while they bemoan the 'unnatural' character of many woods.

By neolithic times it seems probable that about 50 per cent of the British Isles was covered with climax woodland of one sort or another: it is a sobering thought that by the middle of this century woodland cover represented only a mere 6 per cent. Admittedly, this figure has changed a little in the last two decades, with the growth of afforestation, but the fact remains that man managed to clear away the greater part of our woodlands over a very short period of time.

Woodland was cut down and the timber used for various domestic purposes by these early men; some of it was burned down. The cleared areas were then taken over by the first small agricultural plots and to a great extent also by cattle and sheep, which by grazing effectively prevented any natural regeneration. There was a marked preference for clearing the more fertile, better-drained areas—thus wet lower-lying parts of valleys would be avoided, along with heavy clays, peatlands and infertile sandy soils. Equally, steep slopes and rocky terrain would be avoided as difficult to work. Quite possibly it was simply easier to tackle beech woodland than oak forest in any case. It was probably during this period that the first real movement out of the woodlands by birds exploiting the new, open habitats started to take place, involving species like crows, jackdaws and starlings.

With the arrival of the Iron Age came even greater pressures on woodland as more and more wood was needed for smelting, and charcoal assumed great importance. So the rate of clearance accelerated, becoming particularly extensive in important iron-smelting areas such as the Weald of Kent and Sussex and the Forest of Dean, but also occurring on a large scale in more 'remote' areas such as the Lake District and western Scotland: compared with what had gone before, the devastation must have been enormous in some areas. Burning probably took place on site very often. There is also good reason to suppose that some wholesale clearances of woodland took place simply to protect settlements and their livestock from wolves and other potential predators. The rate of clearance was stepped up yet again in the last century before the birth of Christ as new settlers from Europe arrived with bigger and more effective ploughs—which incidentally enabled them to get to grips with the lower-lying, heavier soils of the lowlands where oak forest was dominant. The impetus was maintained through the settled era of the Roman occupation, increasing yet again as new waves of European invaders arrived from the fifth century onwards. Interestingly, woodlands on the drier uplands may actually have made some slight comeback during this period as the older, higher settlements were abandoned in favour of those on lower ground—but the difference this made to the overall trend must have been only very slight. By Saxon times things were changing once more: larger areas of land came under the plough as the rotational 'three-field system' brought bigger agricultural units into being; the Danes more or less carried on this general trend during the time they held sway. Just before the Norman Conquest, perhaps as much as 75 per cent of the former forest and woodland cover had been cleared.

Early in medieval times the first attempts at some sort of preservation of forest remnants came about with the creation of a series of Royal Forests set aside as hunting preserves, complete with their own laws. Several fragments of these forests remain, of which the New Forest is probably the most famous, although others included the forests of Windsor, Dean, Sherwood and Arden. Another interesting development was the creation of 'parks' with deer, which often included remnants of original forest in their boundaries.

Each village or settlement needed a nearby source of timber both for construction work and for fuel, but since the areas nearest the villages were those where the main cultivation took place the woods would be situated some little way from the village itself, often perhaps where the soil was poorest or where the very physical nature of the landscape made clearance impractical. It was important, too, to have the source of timber reasonably close at hand—importing timber from other districts would have presented many problems over transportation. The local communities also grazed their sheep, cattle and goats in the local woodland, which led to a more or less complete prevention of natural regeneration on any sort of significant scale. Swine too were grazed from autumn onwards and, while it is sometimes said that they must have helped in spreading oak woodland by treading in acorns as they foraged, the good this did was probably far outweighed by the numbers of tree seeds they actually ate. Despite the preservation of some forest areas, the combined pressures on woodland brought about by timber exploitation and grazing could have combined to bring about the total disappearance of many woods in the long term. As yet, no thought was being given to replanting to replace what must still have seemed an almost permanent resource.

The first real effort towards replacing the swiftly vanishing woodlands was an act passed in Scotland in 1457 which required tenants of the Scottish Crown to replant their lands. This was timely since, even by the twelfth century, much of the forests of the Scottish Lowlands had effectively vanished. Sheep dominated the land-use of the region at that time, and what woodland did remain was only used irregularly so that much of it degenerated into mixed and partly coppiced scrub woodland; the situation was rather similar in the Highlands, where remnants of the old woodlands only survived in some of the remoter areas or on steep hillsides. There was a great increase in the numbers of sheep everywhere from the thirteenth century onwards: huge areas came under grazing as the woollen industry grew in importance and indeed, by the middle of the fourteenth century, it is reckoned that there were actually four times as many sheep here as there were human beings! All this was of course happening at the expense of woodland and timber had actually become a scarce resource. We think of the importation of timber as a modern development, but in fact during the fourteenth century the first boatloads of wood imported from Scandinavia were reaching our shores.

Coppicing has already been mentioned in connection with some of the Scottish woodlands: it really began to develop as a process of woodland management in the fourteenth and fifteenth centuries and was an important development both economically and for wildlife. Coppicing involves the cutting of a growing tree near the ground and leads to 'shooting' by a whole series of new, relatively small stems which could be harvested in due course for use as poles, fenceposts, firewood and so on. (Coppicing is a rotational activity, the length of the cycle varying according to the tree species, but perhaps lasting 10-15 years.) Some woodlands were coppiced in their entirety, while in others 'standards' or wholly untouched trees were left at intervals. These standards were of rather limited use as timber, except for some special requirements such as shipbuilding, but from a wildlife point of view they added diversity and maintained a mature element in an otherwise strictly managed situation. Interestingly, many coppiced woodlands were also hedged, also adding to their diversity but in more practical terms preventing grazing animals from getting at the new shoots of the cut trees. The coppiced woods brought in more light to the ground flora, enriching it for the first few years of the cycle until the new shoots grew and thickened together; they also encouraged the formation of a good shrub layer in woodlands—the whole proving attractive to various plants and insects and also to some birds, for example nightingales and garden warblers. The tree species involved in coppicing were oak, ash, alder, hornbeam, hazel, and, later, sweet chestnut, and some good examples of coppiced woodland can still be seen—for example, Epping Forest (hornbeams) and Burnham Beeches (beeches).

Another new practice which dates from this period is pollarding: this is basically similar to coppicing, except that the heads of the trees are lopped off some way above the ground. Shooting again takes place, but with the new shoots being larger and thicker than those formed by coppicing (in fact almost resembling slender, subsidiary trunks in some trees). This produces a similar cyclic crop of timber, but with larger dimensions. Because the new shoots were well above ground, they were safe from grazing animals, and thus the formation of hedges is not generally associated with this form of managed woodland. Pollarded trees are often very susceptible to holes forming in them—providing useful homes for a wide range of birds, including tits, redstarts, pied flycatchers and tree sparrows and even some larger species such as owls and stock doves.

Ireland, too, progressively lost much of its extensive forest in the period following the Norman Conquest. Perhaps the greatest devastation occurred during the English Civil War, which imposed a great drain on timber resources in England—so much so that wood was imported from Ireland: here too a crisis point was almost reached by the end of the seventeenth century when Ireland's forest cover had been reduced to virtually nothing. However, a new phase developed from around 1700 to about 1850, when many Irish landlords were encouraging more and more planting on their lands in many parts of the country, while after a somewhat slower start landowners in England and Scotland began to follow suit. The eighteenth century was an important period for widespread planting by enlightened landowners, especially around their great houses and on their large estates. Deciduous trees were often involved, including in the uniquely British form of open 'parkland' which has since become very important for a wide range of wildlife. Pines, too, were planted quite widely, and this period saw the main introduction of a number of alien or exotic trees, important among them being Norway spruce and European larch. The provision of new timber resources and of shelter were not the only considerations now—scenic values were taken into account, and also sporting interests. But while all this was going on, in many areas the old practice of grazing in woodland continued, so that natural regeneration was still held very much in check.

The second half of the eighteenth century, particularly while 'Farmer George' (George III) was on the throne, saw a great leap forward in agriculture—what has since been called the 'Agricultural Revolution'. One of the features which affected trees and woodland birds in particular was the great increase in 'enclosures'—the breaking up of units of agricultural land into fields enclosed by hedges. In fact, enclosure had been going on to some extent ever since medieval times, but it reached its climax during this late period, giving rise to the patchwork of fields and hedges which characterise so much of the British countryside—although, in the north and west and on higher ground, stone walls are more common than hedgerows. While hedges were kept under control to a greater or lesser extent, many hedgerow trees were allowed to grow to full maturity: this network of hedgerow shrubs and mature trees, together with a network of small woods and copses and shelterbelts that grew up along with them, provided an important secondary habitat for many birds. During the preceding centuries many species must have adapted to changing conditions little by little, but now birds such as blackbirds, thrushes, robins, dunnocks, wrens and chaffinches were able to take full advantage of the new habitat provided for them. It is interesting to note just how many mature hedgerow trees there were—in 1951 the Forestry Commission estimated that these accounted for no less than 20 per cent of our mature timber resources! Sadly, the last few decades have seen the wholesale removal of many hedges (and their trees) in many parts of

England, especially in the east where arable farming is dominant: increasing mechanisation and the desire to work larger single-field units have radically altered the face of the countryside, with sometimes disastrous effects on birds and other wildlife.

Although planting continued well into the middle of the nineteenth century, the rate slowed down to a marked degree; nevertheless, more estates and parks were planted and some important new woodlands arose. For instance, part of the Forest of Dean was planted extensively with oak to provide new timber for ships after the Napoleonic Wars; today, 160 years later, we see a fine, mature oak forest which, while it was in fact managed over a long cycle for its timber, was never needed for wooden-walled warships. This century was also important for the arrival of more exotic species which were to become important 100 years or more later: these included Douglas fir, Sitka spruce and Japanese larch. The Industrial Revolution consumed vast amounts of timber, even though oak was increasingly being replaced by iron for construction. Once again there was a long phase of extensive clearance and devastation in many parts of the country, and timber imports increased markedly. To a very small degree, continued planting did something to redress the balance—but not enough. In Ireland, a new threat to those woodlands which remained arose when tenant farmers were enabled to buy up their land. This they did, only to fell and exploit much of the timber it contained.

The nineteenth century saw one more phenomenon which involved woodland very closely—its preservation and management for sporting purposes. This was the period of the rise of the great sporting estates, with their carefully preserved woods and copses. Sportsmen can (and very often do) make the claim that they were responsible for preserving much valuable wildlife habitat that might otherwise have disappeared, and in many lowland areas in particular this would have to include important patches of woodland. Nevertheless, they must also take the full blame for the worst excesses of the 'vermin era' when, armed with increasingly effective shotguns, gamekeepers set out to exterminate anything which could remotely interfere with their gamebirds. Birds of prey and owls in particular were slaughtered in such incredible numbers that it is always a source of great wonder to people today that any of them survived. Some like the goshawk and honey buzzard did not, while another, the red kite, only survived in remote uplands of central Wales. The buzzard population has never fully recovered from this age of slaughter. To some extent, the vermin era continues even to this day—but this is a subject we shall come back to at the end of this book.

By 1900, much of the woodland that had survived all these long centuries of pressure, and of course much of the 'new' planted woodland, were in private hands. One more huge drain on our timber resources was still to come, the First World War. After that, there was a final awakening to the fact that something should be done to replace all the lost timber, and in 1919 the Forestry Commission was formed. What happened next takes us into the era of modern conservation of woodland, with all its problems: this too is considered in the final part of this book.

What we have seen, over a period spanning four millennia since man began to have an impact on woodland, is the survival of woodland from post-glacial times being largely a matter of chance, or more simply because man was unable to get at it for more than short periods at a time. Excepting perhaps a few tiny pockets in remote corners of these islands, there is no true 'original' woodland left. Even where there is a continuous history of woodland for many, many centuries on one site, it has, at one time or another, been modified by man, who may have felled and then replanted it, or changed its species composition. For the most part, we can only have an approximate idea of what the great climax forests of the post-glacial period looked like. It is true that there was some natural regeneration, often in areas where there was a marked alteration in land-use, for example on the steeper slopes of the North and South Downs and in parts of the Peak District—but these too have been touched by the hand of man at some time.

Our look at the history of woodland has been necessarily brief, but it should at least provide the background to the next section of this book, where we look at the nature of the woodland itself and, in particular, at the birds that live in it.

The Woodlands of the British Isles

What is a 'woodland', and how should we set about producing some simple form of classification so that we can consider the distribution of the various kinds of woodland in these islands? The answer to the first part is not quite as simple as it would seem at first: broadly speaking, any aggregation of trees covering an area of five acres could conveniently be classed as a wood. The dividing line between a 'wood' and a 'forest' is highly subjective and no clear-cut distinction has ever been agreed, but in very general terms forests come into being when woodland covers very large areas and is essentially continuous, so that in our islands today, there can be very few true 'forests' left, if one excludes the often vast new conifer plantations which have appeared in some regions. There are some notable examples, of course, such as the New Forest, but equally often we find much smaller fragments still retaining the title 'forest' as a reminder of the days when the area they covered was far greater.

Whatever the dividing line, woodland and forest are often easily identifiable as such, but since we are looking at the picture from the point of view of woodland birds we must not ignore the wide variety of other, subsidiary habitats in which trees are important components—copses, shelterbelts, hedgerows with trees, parkland, large gardens, orchards, scrub with scattered trees—and so on. Woodland birds use all these habitats—and are indeed often more abundant in some of them than in woodland proper.

The answer to our second question, concerning classification, is rather harder to find. There is so much variation in the structure of woods, and in the interrelationships between the trees and the subsidiary 'layers' of woods, that no simple system suggests itself. Equally, further variations are provided by factors such as geographical location, climate, topography, soil conditions and the past and present activities of man. However, although a great many mixed woods exist, dominance by a single tree species is the rule in most British and Irish woodlands, so our best method will be to look at our woods in terms of their dominant species. This means, first of all, looking at the tree layer itself, this being the main component of any woodland and the one which exerts the most influence over the other layers within the wood. It is that part of the wood over 16 feet (5 metres) in height and forming the canopy. Next we shall mention the shrub layer, the part of the wood below 16 feet (5 metres), containing not only shrubs but also young trees; this is often of considerable importance to woodland birds. Finally, we must also mention the field layer, which contains the flora of the woodland, and the ground layer below that.

Theoretically, an ideal woodland would have a very varied and mixed structure, with the three layers above ground all well represented. It would include a wide range of age classes of trees, from self-sown saplings down in the field layer, through to young trees in the shrub layer to semi-mature and mature specimens in the tree layer. It would also include dead and dying trees, even where these have fallen—all are part of the natural life cycle of a woodland. We would expect to see the height and rate of growth of the trees governed by such things as depth and type of soil, exposure, moisture and so on. Unfortunately, such 'ideal woodland' is all too uncommon, thanks largely to man's activities.

Woodland dominated by oak is more widespread than any other kind. There are two species: the pedunculate oak and the sessile oak. Broadly speaking, pedunculate oak is dominant in southern and eastern Britain and is replaced by sessile oak in the west and north—but there are in fact a great many exceptions to this generalisation, as there are to the other generalisation that pedunculate oak favours richer soils, such as those found in the south and east. To complicate matters still further, both species also occur together quite frequently, even hybridising, and pedunculate oak is often the species chosen for planting schemes and commercial woodlands.

Many other species may be found mixed with oak. Among them are ash and wych elm, which may be present in large quantities and take over as dominants on the more calcareous soils: ash is often numerous on calcareous soils in southern and eastern England and is often the dominant species in woods in the west and north, extending well to the north-west of Scotland. Deciduous woodland in the south may also contain varying quantities of several other trees, including small-leaved lime, wild cherry (gean) and English and smooth elms. The last, however, are not often found as dominant woodland trees and are probably better known as hedgerow species. Their abundance and distribution has been affected drastically during the last decade or so by a particularly severe outbreak of Dutch elm disease, which has led to widespread clearance of these fine trees. Interestingly, dead and dying elms are, in the short term at least, good for a variety of insect-eating birds, especially woodpeckers.

Field maple is another plentiful species in southern mixed woodlands, along with the alien sweet chestnut and wild service tree. Hornbeam is a common woodland tree in south-east England, often sharing dominance with oak even though it is usually found as coppice rather than naturally mature timber. Holly and rowan are often present, too, although the former is not often found in large tree form and is usually more typical of the shrub layer than the tree layer. Yew may often occur in small clumps, or occasionally as the dominant species in small woods on the chalk of the North and South Downs; it is also commonly found on calcareous soils in the north up to the Lake District. Other species include aspen, and several alien poplars, crab apples and a wide variety of other aliens such as Turkey oak, horse chestnut, sycamore, the larches, Norway and Sitka spruces, several pines and various firs. Two of these are of particular interest—larch because it spreads freely and grows quickly, and is usually regarded as one of the few aliens which is 'good' for birds, and sycamore, which is highly invasive and may establish partial dominance in some woods. Sycamore is not highly regarded as a good tree for wildlife and on most nature reserves it is actively controlled or widely removed.

Some willows grow to become really large trees, but they are usually found along river banks rather than in woodland. Nevertheless, grey willow in particular may well attain a fair size in the damper parts of woodland, where it often forms a mixed 'carr' with alder. Alder is a very widespread species, used by a great many small birds, wherever the soil is waterlogged. It seldom forms large woods on its own, but tends to occur with willows and birches in carr situations or to form narrow belts of trees along river banks, ditches, etc.

Beech, too, may occur in mixed woodland, sometimes in substantial quantities, but is also forms pure beechwoods, especially in southern England and particularly on thin chalk and limestone soils or on acidic, sandy or gravelly soils. Generally speaking, beechwoods are characterised by their very dense canopies which allow very little light through to the lower parts of the wood when they are in full leaf: for this reason the shrub and field layers are often poor or non-existent, leading to a relatively poor bird fauna. Mixed deciduous woodlands, especially those with a high oak content, are usually the richest in birds, partly because their structure allows the formation of good shrub and field layers.

Scots pine is widespread in many areas of Britain, often forming quite substantial woods or belts of trees, but south of the Scottish Highlands it is generally regarded as an introduced rather than a native species. It does particularly well on poor, acid soils, where it probably represents the climax woodland. A number of fragments of the only remaining natural pine forest—the 'Old Caledonian Forest'—survive in parts of the Highlands, most notably on Deeside and Speyside, and around the Beauly River, but the total area left today is only a few thousand acres, so that this old native pine forest is one of the most threatened types of woodland in Britain.

Birch often replaces pine as the dominant species on the better soils in the Highlands, sometimes sharing dominance with rowan and often forming quite substantial birchwoods. Birch is, of course, a very widespread tree, but south of the Highlands it is essentially a pioneer species on newly-cleared or neglected land, except in a few upland areas. Although it may sometimes form small woods, and while fine mature trees often survive, it is usually replaced in the succession towards climax woodland by oak, beech and other trees. There are two main species of birch—silver birch and downy birch—which are more or less eastern and western species respectively, although there is much overlapping with intermediate forms occurring frequently.

The foregoing is largely a general description of the woodland scene in England, Scotland and Wales. In Ireland, which has only about half as much woodland as the rest of the British Isles, a broadly similar range of species and woodland types exists, although often in scattered, small pockets. Commercial conifers are considered later—but in passing it is worth mentioning that these are increasingly important constituents of the total woodland area in Ireland.

Most of the species we have mentioned, and an even greater variety of exotic aliens, occur outside true woodland, either in small copses or shelterbelts or in parklands, on large estates, in gardens, along streets and so on. In a sense, these form 'subsidiary woodland', or a wide range of secondary habitats for woodland wildlife. They are not readily classified, but they are often of great importance to a wide range of woodland birds and as such must be mentioned in passing.

One important form of woodland remains to be mentioned, namely the widespread and often very large plantations of commercial conifers. They may contain a native species—the Scots pine—but are more often comprised of alien pines, larches, firs and, especially, Norway and Sitka spruces, or indeed a mixture of several of these. They are characterised by their regular rows of trees, planted very close together, often in enormous numbers over huge areas, and by their lack of any form of shrub or field layer, except around firebreaks and 'forest roads'. They are fast becoming the dominant form of woodland in some parts of Britain and Ireland and are increasing in number; they are also highly controversial as far as wildlife and conservation are concerned. In the final part of this book, we shall look at them and their birds again, but for the moment we will only observe that they are perhaps most useful to birds when the plantations are very young.

The richness of woodland in terms of its bird population is often closely tied to the nature of its shrub layer, that part of the wood below 16 feet (5 metres) which includes not only young trees but also various shrub species. Birds use this zone a great deal for feeding, either on insects or fruits, and for nesting, and may have substantial roosts where the cover is thick enough. Very broadly speaking, the richest woods for birds are those with a fairly open form of shrub layer; those where the shrubs are thick and impenetrable, and those where the layer does not exist at all, are generally much poorer.

Much the same sort of factors govern the nature of the shrub layer as the tree layer—climate, soil type and so on and, of course, management by man. As well as restricting natural regeneration of the trees themselves, grazing in woodland can severely inhibit the development of a shrub layer, or completely prevent its appearance—poor or almost non-existent shrub layers are typical of many hill woods of pine, birch and oak. Another limiting factor is imposed by the trees themselves, that of shade: the denser the canopy, the poorer the shrub layer. It is often virtually absent under beech, for instance.

A wide range of species make up the shrub layer, but hazel is probably the most widespread especially on the richer soil types. It often grows in association with oak, where it is frequently in coppice form and produces a fairly dense shrub layer, and is also very typical of western and northern ashwoods. It sometimes forms its own scrubby, semi-woods if the mature trees have been removed. Other abundant species include hawthorn, blackthorn, elder, guelder-rose, various wild roses and bramble—the last often being an important and widespread member of the shrub community which is much used by birds. Hawthorn is also of interest as a pioneer species, especially where grazing is lessened on open areas which will form considerable scrublands which may persist long after the first tree colonists have moved in. Holly and rowan are both often found in woodland shrub layers and are much used by birds, for shelter and food respectively.

On chalk and limestone soils, spindle, whitebeam, dogwood and buckthorn are among the species present. Juniper occurs in the more open pine and birch woodlands in the north, although very often these kinds of woodland lack any real shrub layer. When conditions become wetter, willows and sallow appear, locally with alder buckthorn, often forming carrs with alder. In some situations bog myrtle may attain shrub proportions and high densities. One species which remains to be mentioned is the widely-planted, alien and highly invasive rhododendron, an attractive enough shrub, especially when flowering, but one which woodland conservationists often actively remove because it is very poor in insects, casts a very deep shade and forms dense, impenetrable thickets which are only of very limited value to wildlife.

The field layer and the ground layer, with their small shrubs, herbs, grasses, ferns and so on are likewise dependent on a variety of natural and man-induced factors, as well as on the nature of the tree and shrub layers. We need not go into the detail of their varied composition here, but should mention that the floor of a wood provides many feeding and nesting opportunities for woodland birds: again, we can say that the more varied and luxuriant this zone is, the better it will be for birds.

Woodland Birds

Having spent some time examining the history and nature of our woodlands, we must now turn to the birds themselves and see how they use this type of habitat—but first, a few general comments must be made on the density and diversity of species.

While there is much local and regional variation, we can generalise by stating that, on average, mixed woodland has the highest numbers of birds; broadleaved woodland is only slightly less well populated, but has twice as many birds per acre as natural coniferous woodland. At the very bottom of the scale come the dense, even-aged conifer plantations. Interestingly, built-up areas, especially those with a mosaic of gardens and plenty of trees, are generally as good as mixed woodlands, while parks may have twice as many birds living in them. There is a general rule in nature that diversity increases with size, and this is very often what happens in woodland: bigger woods will tend to have more varied populations than smaller ones. But diversity also decreases as we go north in Britain, so that southern woodlands contain a much greater variety of species than those of the far north: the extremes are about 75 species in the New Forest and as few as 15 in some woods in the far north-west of Scotland.

Our next task is to define a 'woodland bird'—which is not quite as straightforward as might first seem to be the case. Different people have produced different definitions, but here we shall only consider those birds which have some regular connection with woods (or trees) during at least some part of the year. This would exclude some species which may well be seen regularly in woodland, but in fact have no direct connection with the woodland itself—examples might be kingfishers on ponds and streams in lowland woods (even though they will use tree branches over the water to fish from!), or dippers on fast-flowing streams in the west and north. Even so, some waterbirds *do* need to be included, as we shall see, and our total list will come to over 100 species—more than any other type of habitat could muster. About one-third of these are 'real' woodland birds: others have a partial association with trees or woods; some are versatile enough to occur in many other habitats too. In the chapter 'A Selection of Species' later in this book, fifty of these species have been selected for detailed treatment and illustration, for various reasons, as mentioned in the introduction to that chapter.

Among these waterbirds are herons which are not normally thought of as woodland birds, but many of them nest in colonies of varying size in both deciduous and coniferous woods or clumps of trees, building large stick nests in the treetops. The largest heronry, with over 200 pairs, is at the Royal Society for the Protection of Birds (RSPB) reserve at Northward Hill, in Kent; these birds moved down from oak woodland into an area of pure, mature elm, but following the devastation caused by Dutch elm disease have now returned again to the oakwood. Ducks, too, seem unlikely birds to occur in woods, unless there are ponds, rivers or lakes, but mallard often nest in the cover of the field layer in broadleaved woods, in scrub and sometimes even in trees; I have found teal nests in mixed birch and juniper woodland in the Highlands, and have even seen a gadwall with small ducklings in a mature English oakwood. Shelduck seldom nest right inside woods, but may use rabbit burrows around wood edges and rides, or nest in large tree-holes or among the roots of big old trees. The red-breasted merganser also nests around the fringes of woods, in deep cover, but its close relative, the goosander, is a tree-nester, using large holes, deep fissures or large hollow limbs, normally near water and seldom far inside a wood. Another tree-nester is the goldeneye, a common breeding bird in northern Scandinavia but only recently established as a regular breeder in small numbers in the Scottish Highlands: goldeneye will use natural holes in trees, but in Scotland has been tempted to use large, specially-constructed nestboxes of the kind which are widely used in Scandinavia.

Another duck which nests in holes in trees is the introduced mandarin duck, an eastern Asian exotic which has been at large in southern England for 50 years and has now been admitted officially to the British list. Its stronghold is in Surrey and Berkshire, but there are others scattered across the southern half of England and also on the Tay near Perth: most of the ones away from the main concentrations are within reach of waterfowl collections. Old trees with suitable nesting holes are needed by mandarins and they, too, take readily to nestboxes if provided, as does their close American cousin, the wood duck, which is also at large and breeding ferally in a few localities in England, though not yet in sufficient numbers to have become properly established. It too looks for suitable nest-sites in old, decaying trees.

As the text on specific species shows, both sparrowhawks and buzzards are woodland nesters, but they are by no means the only birds of prey to be associated with woods and trees. Our commonest bird of prey, the kestrel, uses holes in trees or old crows' nests—although these are usually on the fringes of woods, along hedgerows, in copses and shelterbelts rather than in deep woodland. A much rarer falcon, the hobby, breeds in old crows' nests for the most part, mainly in Scots pine and normally in isolated clumps of trees, shelterbelts and tall hedgerow trees, but sometimes near the edge of a wood or plantation. It is principally a bird of open country, largely confined to England south of a line from the Bristol Channel to the Wash, with an entire population probably not much over 100 pairs.

The goshawk, on the other hand, is a real woodland bird, nesting in either broadleaved trees or conifers. It closely resembles the sparrowhawk in form and habits, but is far larger and takes much bigger prey—birds as big as crows, woodpigeons and pheasants, and a range of mammals, including both red and grey squirrels in woodland. I even know of one goshawk which 'took over' a small pinewood from a pair of sparrowhawks, simply by eating them! The goshawk vanished to all intents and purposes from the whole of Britain following massive human persecution in the nineteenth century, but the full details of its disappearance are unknown. Similarly, we really know very little about the quite spectacular comeback it is making now in many well-wooded or recently afforested areas in Scotland, England and Wales, and whether any natural recolonisation is taking place. It seems very likely that virtually all the goshawks now living in these areas escaped from falconers or were deliberately released by them—or are descended from such birds. At any rate, pairs are now breeding freely in many areas, often thanks to their extreme furtiveness in the nesting season. The honey buzzard, on the other hand, remains one of our rarest breeding birds of prey: there are probably not more than 10 pairs in a handful of deciduous woodlands in the southern half of England. It may never have been particularly numerous in the past, but it certainly declined during the 'vermin era'. It needs a mixture of mature broadleaved woodland and open spaces, and is unique among European birds of prey for its habit of feeding mainly on the ground on bees, wasps, their larvae, honeycombs and so on.

The red kite was once very widespread, but after virtual extermination now survives only in central Wales, with a population of around 30 pairs which has grown very, very slowly after about 80 years of constant and conscientious protection. Its classic nesting habitat is the 'hanging' sessile oakwood of Welsh upland valley hillsides— a habitat which is threatened in several ways (including by commercial forestry which could replace some of it) and jealously preserved and fought for by conservationists. The other menace facing the kite also comes from commercial forestry, which is an increasing threat to the upland sheep-walks which are the principal feeding areas of this fine bird. Another raptor (bird of prey), the osprey, was totally exterminated from its last strongholds in the Scottish Highlands early in this century—but it has made a dramatic return in the last 25 years and, helped by much protection and beneficial publicity, has gradually built up its numbers to about 20 pairs today: the osprey story is one of the best-known and most exciting in modern bird conservation. Ospreys nest principally in mature Scots pines, normally in open forest in the Highlands or in isolated trees.

Four more birds of prey must be mentioned, although none of them is in any sense a true woodland bird. The smallest British species, the merlin, just scrapes into the list because a small number breed in scattered small trees in some areas in sheltered gullies and the like on open moorland, using old crows' nests—but it is mainly a ground-nester of open country. The largest species, the golden eagle, has better qualifications: a small proportion of our 250 – 300 pairs nest regularly in trees, mainly old, stunted Scots pines on hillsides or in little side-glens but sometimes at the edge of pine woodland proper; commercial plantations are usually avoided, but I knew of one nest in a rectangular block of Scots pines. Oak has also been used in at least one area. Montagu's harrier has all but vanished as a British breeding species, but it has been known to nest in young conifer plantations—a new type of habitat much favoured by its close relative, the hen harrier, a bird which was one restricted to Orkney but has now spread widely in Scotland and also into England and Wales in the wake of increasing afforestation. For a few years, these infant woodlands provide ideal nesting and feeding habitats for hen harriers and this species has unquestionably benefited enormously from the great spread of commercial forestry in the last few decades—even though this does at the same time gobble up much feeding habitat on moors and marginal land. What will happen when the pace of planting slows down and when today's young plantations grow too tall and too dense for harriers remains to be seen. At some stage, which must come fairly soon in the older forests, clear-felling and replanting may begin the cycle all over again: it will be very interesting to see if, and how, the harriers adapt.

One partial woodland gamebird, the pheasant, and one rather special gamebird of the old Scottish pine forests, the capercaillie, feature in the chapter on specific species. Another, the black grouse, is often found in open birch and pine woodland, or where this adjoins open moorland, and in young conifer plantations, where it feeds on the new shoots of the young trees. The males, or blackcocks, are well known for their spectacular communal displays or 'leks'; like capercaillies, black grouse also habitually perch in trees. They are widespread in suitable habitat in Scotland, but are rather less common in northern England and are either uncommon or really rare in their other main habitats in Wales, the Pennines, Exmoor and Dartmoor. Two introduced gamebirds, in which the males have particularly exotic plumage, are both true forest or woodland species with well-established small populations: the golden pheasant from central China breeds in parts of East Anglia, in south-west Scotland, on Anglesey and in a few other scattered localities, while Lady Amherst's pheasant, known affectionately to many birdwatchers as 'Lady A's P', which comes from south-west China, Tibet and upper Burma, is fully naturalised in a few areas in south-eastern England, principally in Bedfordshire, Buckinghamshire and Hertfordshire. Both species show a distinct preference for coniferous woods and plantations.

Lady Amherst's Pheasant

The moorhen is essentially a waterbird, often found in parks and woods, but it has some claim to inclusion on our list because it sometimes nests in big bushes or even small trees, either in woods or alongside water, and because it may wander some distance from water to feed on the woodland floor. Of the wading birds, the woodcock is the only true woodland species; however, the wood sandpiper, which has a very small breeding population in the Scottish Highlands, deserves a mention because it sometimes nests in trees in open woodlands near wetlands, using the old nests of other birds—although, to the best of my knowledge, this habit has not so far been recorded in Scotland. Equally, another Highland species, the greenshank, might just qualify for a mention here because it sometimes nests well inside pine woodlands; in northern Scandinavia, I have often seen greenshanks 'singing' from the tops of high trees.

The collared dove, unknown in Britain until 25 years ago, is not generally encountered in true woodland, but is now a well-known bird of well-timbered parks and gardens. Its spectacular spread westwards across Europe hit Britain in 1955: today it is an extremely common bird over virtually all of Britain and Ireland wherever even the smallest pocket of suitable habitat exists—e.g., even at remote farms in otherwise open country. The cuckoo occurs in almost every conceivable type of habitat away from built-up areas and is a typical summer bird of open woodland edges and other places where there are scattered trees. Cuckoos are well known as 'brood parasites' and may victimise quite a wide range of small woodland birds, although only the dunnock qualifies for this doubtful distinction with any real regularity.

All of the five regular breeding British owls have some connection with woodland or trees, even if only the tawny and long-eared are real woodland birds. Little owls and barn owls use scattered trees and hedgerow trees when these have suitable nesting holes, and the former sometimes occurs well inside woods, though the barn owl is really a bird of open country. The short-eared owl's association with woodland is only with very young conifer plantations: in essence it closely parallels the hen harrier in this respect. In the main species accounts the nightjar has been included as an example of a group of birds which are colonists of new plantations. It is among the first birds to use these new habitats, and among the first to pull out once the young trees grow too tall. It also favours wide rides and firebreaks, clearings and felled area in woodland, as well as the open heathland which is usually its main habitat.

The three typical woodpeckers are obvious woodland birds. A fourth species, the wryneck, might not be recognised as a woodpecker at all when seen. It is a beautifully patterned brown, grey and buff sparrow-sized bird, not often seen actually climbing on tree trunks like the other woodpeckers, and it is frequently encountered feeding on the ground where, like the green woodpecker, it is particularly fond of ants. It is also a summer migrant and, unlike the other species, nests in natural holes in trees rather than in holes it has exacavated itself. Wrynecks may nest in true woodland, usually in fairly open areas, but they are more characteristic of parkland with scattered trees, old orchards and large gardens. Once they nested as far north as Durham and the Lake District and westwards into Wales, being commonest and most widespread in central and south-eastern England, but since about

1830 they have been in decline; this decline accelerated during the 1960s and by the 1970s the species had all but disappeared as an English breeding bird. To most birdwatchers today, it is much more familiar as an autumn migrant at the coast. The reasons for this decline are far from clear, but are probably connected with a long-term deterioration in summer weather. However, since the 1960s an extraordinary thing has happened: wrynecks have appeared in the Scottish Highlands and are now nesting regularly in small numbers. These birds must be colonists from Scandinavia, one of a number of northern species which have started to breed in Scotland in recent decades and part of a trend which must also be related to long-term climatic change. Interestingly, lesser spotted woodpeckers have also recently appeared in Scotland, well to the north of their normal range in Britain, posing the question of whether they too might be northern colonists.

Two rather exotic species which are widely distributed in continental Europe are woodland birds. The spectacular hoopoe, a pinkish-brown bird with an extravagant crest and strikingly black-and-white wings and tail, is a hole-nesting bird of open woodland, parkland, large gardens and areas with scattered trees, which nests here irregularly, usually in southern England. The secretive golden oriole,

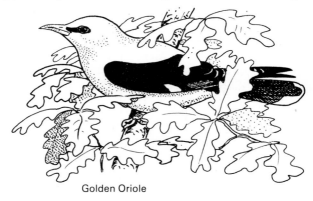

Golden Oriole

which, despite the fact that the male is brilliantly golden-yellow and black (the female is greener), is one of the hardest of all woodland birds to see, is usually first located by its loud, fluty song. On the Continent it breeds in a variety of woodlands, from mature broadleaved to damp carr and riverside forest; it has bred in a rather irregular way in England in the past, and once in Scotland but has now established itself quite firmly as a new colonist in one or two areas in the southern half of England.

Larks, like pipits, are essentially birds of open country, not generally associated with trees, but one species, the woodlark, occurs in areas with a combination of open grassland and either scrub or scattered trees, or, in some areas, along the margins of woodlands. It is of interest as yet another bird which occurs in young forestry plantations, generally having arrived there initially when the previous tree cover has been clear-felled. After various fluctuations in numbers and distribution in England and Wales, woodlarks have declined quite widely, partly no doubt due to loss of habitat but also probably as a result of climatic change. Woodlarks are quite similar in appearance to the much more familiar skylark, but have very short tails, without white outer feathers, and conspicuous creamy eyestripes. Their beautifully rich song, delivered in a high song-flight or from a perch (often high in a tree) is thought by many to be one of the finest of all.

We have been a little hard on the crow tribe by only including the jay in our list of selected species, even if it is the most woodland-orientated one of all. Years of persecution have pushed the raven to the north and west in mainland Britain and today it is most closely associated with open uplands, mountain country and sea-cliffs, but it must have been a tree-nester when it was common in lowland Britain

Rook

centuries ago. Today it still nests in scattered trees and even in woodlands in parts of Wales and the West Country. The all-black carrion crow is a highly adaptable bird, found in a variety of habitats, but it is essentially a tree-nester and though it feeds mainly in open country, including widely on arable land, it frequently breeds in woods and most other habitat with reasonably tall trees. The grey-and-black hooded crow, not a separate species but in the same one as the carrion crow (with which it interbreeds freely where both occur), occurs in more open, higher ground in the west and north of Scotland, though it too is mainly a tree-nester and will breed in woods where these are available. It replaces the carrion crow almost completely in Ireland. Rooks feed in open, arable country, but nest colonially in trees—in copses, shelterbelts, lines of roadside trees and near the edges of woods, and even in built-up areas. Jackdaws occur in a variety of habitats, but these include woodlands and all sorts of other areas where there are groups of trees; they often breed in colonies and where they use trees they nest in old timber with suitably large holes or crevices—although they may sometimes build 'outside' nests in dense foliage or in ivy. Magpies are not often found far inside woods, but they will nest in the outer edges. They are generally more common in areas of scrub, tall old hedgerows and scattered trees, where they feed mainly on old pastures and poor agricultural land, and also occur frequently in built-up areas where there are parks and large gardens.

Of the small passerines, or perching birds, which remain (tits, thrushes, warblers, finches, etc.) most of those associated in some way with woodland appear in the species accounts, but there are a dozen which require mentioning here. These include two northern thrushes, the redwing and the fieldfare, which are best known as winter migrants

Redwing

from northern Europe but have both appeared here as colonists in recent years. Fieldfares breed in an incredibly wide range of habitats in Europe, including woods, scrub, parks and gardens, and have shown similar tendencies in their scattered and often somewhat irregular nesting places in Scotland and England. Redwings, which breed only in northern Scotland, are similarly catholic in their choice of habitats in Scandinavia; here they have nested in oak and birch woodland, in alders, in shrubs and several other habitats—including some with no trees at all. Of the widespread resident thrushes, the mistle thrush (illustrated with song thrush in the chapter on specific species) is a bird of open woodland or wood edges, and many types of open country with scattered trees—including parks and gardens. It has a special reputation among the smaller British birds in being particularly bold in defence of its nest. Two small relatives, the stonechat and the whinchat, are more birds of young coniferous plantations, but, apart from sometimes using trees as song-posts, are not otherwise associated with woodland in any way.

The little Dartford warbler of the southern heathlands of England is in no way a woodland bird, but young regenerating Scots pines and other trees are often present in its special habitat and while these trees are still small it may well use them for feeding or as song-posts; too much tree invasion on heathland, however, soon leads to the disappearance of this rather rare bird. Both the whitethroat and the lesser whitethroat are essentially birds of hedgerows and scrubby places, though both—the latter in particular—may occur in woodland edges and sing from quite tall trees. The elusive grasshopper warbler, more often heard with its incredible song than seen, the song sounding like the endless unwinding of an angler's reel, is in many areas particularly fond of young conifer plantations, which may well compensate for the loss of many of the wetland habitats in which it also occurs. In common with two other essentially wetland species, the sedge and reed warblers, it is often found in carr and scrub around the edges of marshes.

The red-backed shrike is another declining species in southern and eastern England, again probably due to climatic factors, and also another which has recently nested in Scotland, presumably as a result of colonisation from northern Europe. When it was still tolerably common in southern England (only 30 years ago) it occurred in a variety of scrubby situations, often with scattered trees, in old orchards and gardens and even around wood edges and in large woodland clearings. Today's remnant population is largely confined to heaths with scattered hawthorns or other shrubs and a few scattered trees.

Linnets are principally birds of scrub and hedgerow, but are sometimes among that group of birds which use young conifer plantations. Much the same can be said of the yellowhammer although it features more regularly among the pioneer species of the new habitat. Both species often sing from mature hedgerow trees, which (especially elms) are also particularly important to the cirl bunting in its largely farmland habitat in southern and south-western England. Last, but by no means least, there is the brambling, which more or less replaces the chaffinch in the northernmost part of Europe. It has probably bred occasionally in birch and mixed coniferous woods in Scotland in the recent past, and singing males are encountered somewhere in most summers. It is better known in the British Isles, though, as a winter visitor, where it often appears in mixed finch flocks feeding on farmland and around the edges of woodland. It occurs too in winter flocks with greenfinches, chaffinches and (sometimes) hawfinches deep inside woodlands, where it is particularly well known for its fondness of beechmast.

Hawfinch

Birdwatching

One of the best things about birdwatching is that it can be done almost anywhere, at any time. It need not be an expensive hobby and it can be as relaxing or strenuous as you care to make it. You can do it just for fun or you can take it very seriously indeed. Whichever way you decide, it will give you great pleasure and satisfaction, it could take you to all sorts of exciting places—and it should enable you to meet lots of other like-minded people. Above all, perhaps, it will lead you towards a better understanding and appreciation of the natural world we live in. This is a book about woodland birds—which means the birds of parks, gardens and hedgerows, too—so most of what follows will be written in the context of birdwatching in that sort of habitat. Luckily, most of us have some accessible woodland close to home: it is as good a place to start as any.

What equipment will you need to become a birdwatcher? Not too much, in fact: a reasonably good pair of binoculars is a must (telescopes are not very useful in most woodland situations), as is a notebook. The right sort of clothing can be important, and so are a few good reference books.

Choosing the right pair of binoculars is very much a matter of personal taste, and what you can afford. You can pay several hundred pounds if you really want to for the very best makes, but there are many more priced well under £100 and you should by no means ignore the various low-priced Japanese varieties, some of which can be extremely good. I am still using a pair of Japanese 10 x 50 binoculars bought for me in 1968 for less than £15 which have survived a lot of travelling and rough usage and are still going strong. There is some advantage in having reasonably low-priced binoculars in that they can be replaced fairly painlessly if they are damaged! If you take care of your glasses and keep them clean, there is no reason why they should not last you a lifetime. At any rate, do not be fooled by the birdwatchers you occasionally meet who seem to take a weird delight in owning the newest, biggest and most 'modern' binoculars—they are probably deluding themselves in believing that these are what is best to be seen with!

There is a bewildering variety of binoculars available. The best bet is to shop around, trying out as many different pairs as possible and choosing whatever suits you best: seek the advice of other birdwatchers if you can. A magnification above 'x 10' is not necessary. If you wear spectacles, make sure that you ask about makes with suitably designed eye-pieces, plenty of which are available. And watch out for binoculars which are very heavy: they can become an incredible burden after they have been hanging round your neck for a couple of hours. On the 'technical' side, you should look for a pair of glasses with a good field of view—especially useful in woodland. Broadly speaking, the field of view decreases as magnification increases, but it also increases with the diameter of the object lens (the one furthest from your eye). Good light-gathering qualities are essential, especially in woodland situations where you are often working in the shade and in dense cover. You can assess the light-gathering potential of a pair of binoculars by doing a simple calculation: every pair of glasses carries a note of its magnification followed by the diameter (in millimetres) of its object lenses, for example, 7 x 50, 8 x 30, 10 x 50 and so on. Divide the diameter of the lens by the magnification and if the answer is below 4 it is probably as well to think again. Unfortunately, very few 7 x 50 binoculars are available nowadays. These are a little low on the magnification side, but their light-gathering power, especially at dusk, is outstandingly good: they are ideal for use in woodland. It is difficult, without a fair amount of experience with binoculars, to assess how good their resolution of detail is, and even how quickly and accurately they come into focus, but by trying out several different pairs in a shop you will get some idea of how they compare—and you could always ask to look through a pair of really expensive ones to obtain a yardstick for the others! Remember to take them *outside* to try them out. Some expert help is preferable before you finally make up your mind. You should avoid any binoculars which produce a bright rainbow effect around the edge of your 'picture'—this is a sure indication that they are optically unsatisfactory. Personally I would also avoid buying binoculars by mail order: I think they are so important to the bird watcher that it is far better to go to a good shop which offers a wide variety of makes which you can handle and try for yourself. 'Zoom' lenses are featured on some makes: for birdwatching, these are unnecessary—and likely to go wrong in any case.

A notebook is essential. The type does not matter too much, although something with a stiff or waterproof cover is probably best. Every birdwatcher who has been out in heavy rain knows how annoying it can be to find a soft-covered or flimsy notebook in his pocket feeling like a wad of wet blotting paper, with his notes blurred or washed out . . . A weatherproof cover, especially one of those which overlaps the edge of the pages, will keep its shape and keep out most of

Date: 15ᵀᴴ June   Location: Abernethy

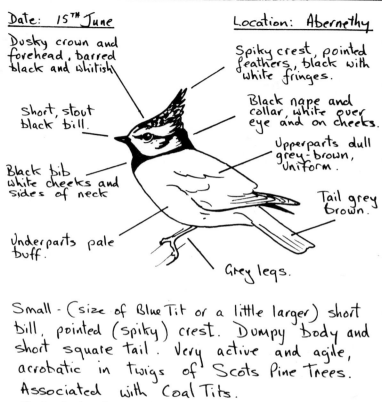

Dusky crown and forehead, barred black and whitish

Spiky crest, pointed feathers, black with white fringes.

Short, stout black bill.

Black nape and collar, white over eye and on cheeks.

Upperparts dull grey-brown, uniform.

Black bib white cheeks and sides of neck

Tail grey brown.

Underparts pale buff.

Grey legs.

Small - (size of Blue Tit or a little larger) short bill, pointed (spiky) crest. Dumpy body and short square tail. Very active and agile, acrobatic in twigs of Scots Pine Trees. Associated with Coal Tits.

Call distinctive - a low trilling note - spluttering - "pt-rrrp". Habitat - Scots Pine and Birch woodland with Heather and Juniper beneath. Kept in low branches. Watched at 15 feet range in good light. 8×40 binoculars. Coal Tit and Blue Tit present for comparison.

Field Reference

the wet, too. Personally, I use one of the several waterproof covers now available with a loose-leaf system of pages: like my old binoculars, my old notebook is an item of practical as well as sentimental value which has been with me for a long time. I find it much easier to put in new pages than to buy new notebooks. It is also cheaper! Some people, however, keep their notebooks as their only permanent record of their observations; others, myself among them, 'write up' from their field notebooks into some form of more detailed record, which can vary from a general diary to highly complicated systems of lists and card-indexes. Really, it is up to the individual to decide what to do, or indeed whether to do it at all. Personally, when I write up my notebooks, I use a diary format in big loose-leaf binders, which allows me plenty of scope to record whatever I like in as much detail as I wish—and also provides good reading and pleasant memories years afterwards.

What to write in a notebook is, again, a matter of personal choice. It can vary from simple lists of birds seen, with numbers, places, etc., to notes on plumage, behaviour, feeding, nesting and so, accompanied by sketches, maps or whatever else is necessary. The real point here is that there are no hard-and-fast rules. I believe, quite simply, that no real naturalist is ever without his notebook.

What clothing you wear for birdwatching obviously depends a great deal on the weather, and is, in any case, largely a matter of personal choice. The golden rule is to be comfortable—how you feel is much more important than how you look, although another good rule is to avoid really bright colours (hats, anoraks, cagoules, etc.): in woodland it is far better to achieve at least some camouflage effect by choosing greens and browns which will help you to blend into your background. Most birdwatchers like to have some sort of outdoor jacket or anorak: this should be dull-coloured, tough, warm (a hood is also useful, both to keep you dry and to serve as camouflage), well provided with pockets and, above all, reasonably waterproof. It is best to avoid many of the lightweight types made from synthetic materials, which can be incredibly noisy in thick cover and, in addition, often tear very easily in woods, where there is often a tangle of low branches, thorns or brambles to be negotiated. The same sort of considerations should be borne in mind with trousers—which, incidentally, are often far more practical for female birdwatchers than skirts: undergrowth can be especially hard on tights and stockings! Jeans are good all-purpose wear, but really anything strong and durable will do. Footwear is very important, especially in cold or wet weather, and again in undergrowth in woodland. Rubber boots are fine, but care needs to be taken over the warmth of your feet—some of the modern 'boot liners', especially those made of quilted nylon filled with polyester, are particularly good. Otherwise, any reasonably robust shoes or boots will do; in summer there is much to be said for the plimsolls still worn by a few birdwatchers of the older generation—or the modern training shoes which have replaced them. Lastly, remember your gloves in winter: apart from having cold or wet feet, there are few things as unpleasant when birdwatching than numb hands and frozen fingers.

The well-equipped birdwatcher

What books will you need for reference purposes? This book will help you to name about half the birds you might encounter in woodland habitats, but others designed purely as identification guides are also needed. There are several of these available: the oldest, and in my view by far the best for its text and illustrations, is the *Field Guide to the Birds of Britain and Europe* (Collins) by Roger Peterson, Guy Mountfort and Philip Hollom. Three others—*The Birds of Britain and Europe, with North Africa and the Middle East* (Collins) by Herman Heinzel, Richard Fitter and John Parslow; *The Hamlyn Guide to the Birds of Britain and Europe* by Bertel Bruun and Arthur Singer; and *The Birdwatcher's Key* (Warne) by Bob Scott and Don Forrest —all offer rather less text, but have all their illustrations appearing opposite the text. All these will go into your pocket. Perhaps their one drawback, especially for the beginner in the British Isles, is that they show all the birds found in Europe. While this is very useful on a Continental holiday, both for woodland birds and those of other habitats, it can sometimes lead to confusion and misidentification of birds seen here, so it is essential to check on where the bird actually occurs before considering it as a possibility. Two other books, both too big for the pocket (see later) and using a different system of illustration in that they show birds 'in action' and as one might see them in life, rather than in portrait form, are *The Birdlife of Britain* (Mitchell Beazley/RSPB) by Peter Hayman and Philip Burton, and *What's That Bird?* (RSPB) by Peter Hayman and myself. There is also a scaled-down version of the first of these, *The Mitchell Beazley Birdwatcher's Pocket Guide*. All are aimed very much at the beginner.

The best general reference book, which will also help you a great deal with identification, is *The Popular Handbook of British Birds* (Witherby) by Philip Hollom. Perhaps the most comprehensive book dealing with the topics in this section, and many more besides, is the *RSPB Guide to Birdwatching* (Hamlyn) by Peter Conder. Worth having a look at, especially the section on woodlands, is the encyclopaedic *Nature Conservation Review* (Cambridge University Press) edited by Dr Derek Ratcliffe; its two volumes should be available at libraries. For a book on natural history observation generally, especially suitable for young people, I can do no better than recommend *Looking at Wildlife* (Beaver Books) by Nicholas Hammond. For woodland specifically, the best reference book is *Woodland Birds* by Eric Simms, in the Collins New Naturalist Series; the best guide to trees is *A Field Guide to the Trees of Britain and Northern Europe* (Collins) by Alan Mitchell, and for woodland plants there is *The Wild Flowers of Britain and Northern Europe* (Collins) by Richard and Alastair Fitter and Marjorie Blamey. There is also another book in this 'Britain's Natural Heritage' series, *The Guinness Book of Wild Flowers* by Mary Briggs, which treats this subject as woodland birds are treated here.

There are literally scores of other books on birds, many of them dealing with aspects of birds in woodland, but those I have mentioned should form the basis of a good 'library'. Again, the aid of a knowledgeable birdwatching friend can be invaluable in deciding which books to buy.

Thus equipped, there comes the actual business of going out to look at birds. I must emphasise again that it is not necessary to make special journeys to see birds, especially in the early stages: visits to major bird reserves, etc. should come later, *after* you have mastered the birds at home, in your local wood, park or garden. Begin locally, get to know your local birds backwards and, above all, remember that successful birdwatching is built on patience and the steady accumulation of experience. There can be no such thing as an 'instant birdwatcher'. All through these early stages, you should read your bird books, referring to them constantly so that you gradually build up your background knowledge. This sort of 'homework' is of great importance and you will be pleasantly surprised at how much of it will stick in your mind when you are in the field.

When looking at birds, get to know their colour patterns and their distinguishing features: do they have wingbars like a chaffinch, a white rump like a bullfinch, or a white tip to the tail like a hawfinch? Note, too, that males and females may have different plumages, and that young birds may be different again. In woodland, you will often only get half-views of birds, perhaps as they fly up from the ground into the trees—but if you have learned your field-marks, this could be all you need. For instance, a brief view of a smallish bird from behind which has broad white wingbars and a white-tipped tail will be all you need to be able to say 'hawfinch' with complete certainty. Many birds will be above you—pay attention to their underparts, heads and tails in particular: a wood warbler flitting in the treetops 50 feet (15 metres) above you shows a unique pattern with its yellow breast and strikingly white belly; you will very often see its bright yellow eyestripe, too.

It is just as important to learn the shapes of birds—they can often be identified by shape and size alone. A silhouetted hawfinch is a case in point: its huge bill, bull neck and short tail could belong to no other woodland bird. Shape in flight is also important—is it long-tailed, and what shape are its wings? Movement is just as vital, both at rest and in the air. Does the bird hop like a robin, shuffle like a dunnock, or walk with the cocksure confidence of a starling? Does it forage acrobatically among small twigs, like a tit or a siskin? Does it climb trees jerkily like a treecreeper, 'hop' up the trunk with the springy action of a woodpecker, or run up, down or sideways with the agility of a nuthatch? In flight, does it fly fast and direct like a starling, or in pronounced undulations like a woodpecker? Perhaps it may soar on broad, widespread wings like a buzzard, or flap and glide like a sparrowhawk, or float and twist this way and that like a nightjar. Shape and movement are every bit as important as colouring and are best learned in the field, and not from bird books.

Another aid to identification is where and when you will find your birds. There is a great deal of overlapping in the choice of habitat among woodland birds, but there are a fair number of useful pointers. For example, you are unlikely to find crossbills in oakwoods, or marsh tits in pine forest. Geographical location should be borne in mind too: it is hardly likely that you will see a tawny owl in Ireland, for instance, or hear a nightingale singing in a Scottish wood, or see a crested tit in the Midlands. The time of year should also be remembered —note which birds are present all the year round and which are summer or winter visitors; others may only pass through your area as passage migrants in spring and autumn.

No bird book ever written, including this one, will ever give you a totally satisfactory guide to the other vital factor in bird identification, that of voice. Bird recordings will help to some extent, notably 'Woodland and Garden Birds' by Eric Simms, available on two LPs or on cassette, and some of the 14 records in the 'Peterson Guide to the Bird Songs of Britain and Europe'—but there is no real substitute for the long process of learning bird songs and calls as you go along. It is every bit as important to *listen* as well as to watch: birds all have their own diagnostic songs, and a wide range of calls which they use in different circumstances for different reasons. Perhaps the best way to learn bird voices is to go out with an experienced birdwatcher who knows them well—the same applies, in fact, to learning your birds by sight. An experienced companion from whom you can learn is worth a dozen bird books or records. All this is particularly vital in woodland—there is much bird-finding to do by ear. There are many species which you might hardly see at all unless you recognised their calls: lesser spotted woodpecker, crested tit and hawfinch are all examples which come to mind.

Fieldcraft is sometimes sneered at by modern birdwatchers, but it pays dividends, especially in difficult habitats like woodland. Learn to move slowly and methodically, avoiding sudden, abrupt movements, and try to merge into your background as far as possible when watching birds. Use the cover provided by vegetation and, especially, tree trunks; try to walk silently, taking special care where there are twigs and branches on the ground. With a little forethought and patience, all these simple tactics can become part of you: you may feel a little self-conscious about this at first, but that hurdle is soon overcome. The quiet, thoughtful, patient observer sees far more birds, in far more satisfactory conditions, than the one who rushes about noisily all over the place. Another good ploy is to sit down in a sheltered spot (overlooking a clearing or a pond or stream, for instance) and watch and wait: this will often pay dividends and give you some surprises. I have encountered difficult creatures like badger and polecat by doing this, as well as plenty of birds: I have had fantastic views of cock capercaillies, courting great spotted woodpeckers and flocks of hawfinches feeding on the ground simply by being prepared to sit down and see what came along.

Remember to use your notebook all the time, not only to record the 1001 interesting observations you will make on various aspects of bird behaviour, but also to write down descriptions of birds you don't recognise. It is important to 'learn the parts' on a bird so that you can make your description accurate (see the illustration on page 48) and you can practise writing field descriptions of birds you know already: try it out on a house sparrow, for instance! Learning how to do this properly takes time, but it is a discipline worth mastering. It is better *not* to take the field guide along, in my view, and to refer to its illustrations in the field: this can lead to many errors and a lot of wishful thinking. It is really better to write your notes (which can include sketches, however crude) on the spot and look up in the book afterwards. This will not only make you a much better and more careful observer, but will stand you in good stead for that inevitable occasion when you don't have the book with you. Two of the identification guides mentioned previously are too big to go into your pocket—one of them, at least, was made that way as a conscious step on the part of the artist and author!

Finally, even though birdwatching alone or with one to two companions is often the most satisfying, it is a good idea to find out about and join your local bird club, natural history society or RSPB members' group; and if there are local evening classes in ornithology, why not go along? It is always useful to meet other people who share your interests and to avail yourself of the opportunity to join them on field trips. What is even more important is that you will also meet people who are experienced and knowledgeable in the art of birdwatching: seek their advice and help as often as possible and you will be surprised not only by their willingness to help you but also at how much you will learn from them. Lastly, never worry if you cannot put a name to every bird you see, or if you make mistakes: that is all part of the fun of birdwatching—and is something which happens to the experts too!

Topography of a bird

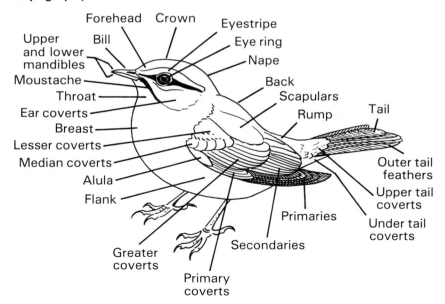

A Selection of Species

Of the birds which are featured in this chapter, I have selected what I consider to be 50 fairly typical species, most of them reasonably common and ones which the average reader should have a fair chance of seeing. A few are either relatively rare, or have limited distributions but, for one reason or another, are interesting in their own right or are appropriate as examples of the surprisingly wide range of birds found in woodlands and associated habitats. Purists may object to the inclusion of the nightjar, perhaps, since it is hardly a woodland bird at all, but it is important to our story since it is one of the first colonists of wholly new commercial conifer plantations and, as such, is thus a pioneer bird in woodlands-to-be. Other readers will also notice some omissions from the selected 50 species: these are all covered, or at least mentioned, in the general section on woodland birds, along with introduced species and some others whose involvement in woodland is only marginal.

Each species in the present section is illustrated by a colour photograph, with additional line drawings by my friend and colleague, Rob Hume: this combination is intended to help with identification and not be merely pictorial! The main features of each species and its way of life are described, together with notes on its status and past and present distribution. Current distribution (and distribution in the past where there has been a marked change) are shown on a series of shaded maps, solid colour indicating that which is current, and diagonal lines indicating that which is past. Much of the information for these maps has been gleaned from the *Atlas of Breeding Birds in Britain and Ireland* by Dr Tim Sharrock and published jointly by the British Trust for Ornithology and the Irish Wildbird Conservancy. It should be noted that the maps in the present book are greatly simplified and are merely intended to show the main limits of distribution, and no attempt has been made to indicate density of numbers, rarity, etc. Obviously any species will only occur where suitable habitats exist within the shaded areas. For local purposes, the reader will find the *Atlas* an invaluable aid.

Buzzard

Buteo buteo

Size: 20 – 23 in (51 – 56 cm).

Recognition: long, broad
wings, short but ample tail and
very short neck. Basically
brown above with varying
amounts of white below,
usually with dark carpal marks
on underwing and narrowly barred
grey and brown tail.

Voice: usual note is a high, mewing
'pee-oo'.

Nesting: builds a large, bulky
nest. Usually 2 – 3 eggs, incubated for
34 – 38 days, the young fledging at 6
or 7 weeks old.

Feeding: hunts small mammals
from vantage points on trees, posts,
etc., or by methodical quartering
flight in open country.

The buzzard is commonest in countryside with
a mosaic of woods, copses and open
farmland, being less numerous (but still
present) in very heavily wooded country or
open moorland and mountains. From being
common over most of Britain and Ireland in
the early nineteenth century it declined due to
very heavy persecution and, by about 1914,
was confined to the extreme west, south
west and north-west of Britain
and had vanished from Ireland.
Reduced persecution and a more
enlightened attitude towards birds
of prey has enabled it to spread
back into many areas in the last
60 years, with some set-backs
following the arrival of
myxomatosis in 1954, but it is
still very much a western and
northern species.

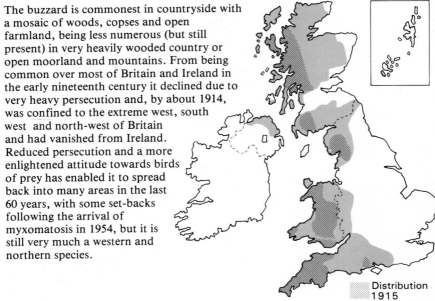

Distribution
1915

Sparrowhawk

Accipiter nisus

Size: 11 – 15 in (28 – 38 cm).

Recognition: small with short rounded wings and a long tail. Male dark blue-grey above, closely barred reddish below; much larger female browner above and whitish below, closely barred with brown.

Voice: usually silent, except at nest, where calls include loud, rapid 'kek-kek-kek', 'keeow', etc.

Nesting: favours conifers. Normally 4 – 5 eggs, incubated by female for up to 35 days, young flying at 24 – 30 days.

Feeding: feeds mainly on small birds with some small mammals and insects.

The sparrowhawk is chiefly a bird of woodland or semi-open country with copses, shelterbelts, parkland, etc., but also occurs in well-timbered suburbs and large gardens. It takes its prey from attacks from perches or by surprise as the sparrowhawk flies through woodland, weaving in and out of cover, or dashes along hedgerows, also pursuing in the open when it often flies down its prey. The sparrowhawk has benefited from the spread of forestry in some regions. In spite of massive and needless persecution by gamekeepers and farmers it was common throughout Britain until the late 1950s and early 1960s when it suffered a great decline through its prey being contaminated by persistent toxic pesticides. With full legal protection since 1963 and the withdrawal of most of these substances it has increased again, but is still rare and local in much of eastern England.

Distribution 1950

Capercaillie

Tetrao urogallus

Size: 34 in (86 cm) male; 25 in (62 cm) female.

Recognition: male is dark grey and brown with whitish bill and ample tail boldly marked with white; smaller female is browner, barred darker, with rufous breast.

Voice: silent, except for hen's occasional loud 'kok-kok' and song of displaying male.

Nesting: in ground vegetation; hen incubates 5 – 8 eggs for about 4 weeks.

Feeding: in summer, leaves, shoots and berries of ground plants; in winter chiefly shoots and buds of conifers.

♂

♀

The capercaillie is essentially a bird of the old, semi-open mature pine forest, but has spread into older plantations, especially where Scots pine is present, and outside the breeding season may move into low-lying mixed woodland and scrub or on to moorland edges. Following the disappearance of most of the natural pine forest in Scotland and Ireland in the eighteenth century, the capercaillie disappeared as a British breeding species around 1785. The present population stems from a series of introductions in the nineteenth century, the largest being Swedish birds into Perthshire in 1837 – 38. So far the reintroduction of the capercaillie into Ireland has not been successful, but attempts are being made to introduce the bird in north-west England.

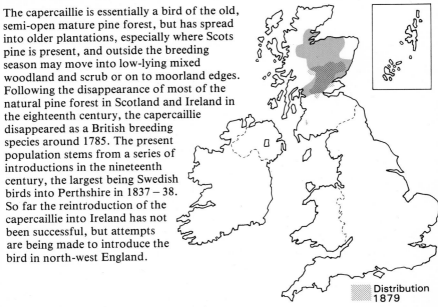

Distribution 1879

Pheasant

Phasianus colchicus

Size: 21 – 35 in (53 – 89 cm).

Recognition: males variable, but mainly copper-coloured, usually with dark green head, always with very long tail. Female much smaller, pale brown marked darker, with rather shorter tail.

Voice: male has loud, far-carrying 'korr-kok', female a quiet whistle.

Nesting: on ground in bramble, long grass, etc. Usually 8 – 15 eggs, incubated by hen for 22 – 27 days. Young leave nest soon after hatching and fly after 2 weeks.

Feeding: feeds on ground; stems, shoots, roots, leaves, seeds, fruits, etc.

The pheasant is an Asian bird and in its original state is a bird of marsh edges and even reed beds as well as scrub and woodland. It was apparently introduced here in Norman times and is now a widespread and familiar gamebird, mainly associated with mixed woodland and farmland but in fact occurring almost anywhere where there is suitable cover. The status of the pheasant is often largely artificial since, in many areas, it is the subject of intensive rearing and release programmes, but even so it is often a very shy and wary bird. Pheasant rearing and gamekeeping have often led to needless persecution of birds of prey and owls, but at the same time have also been responsible for the preservation of much useful habitat in the form of small woods and copses.

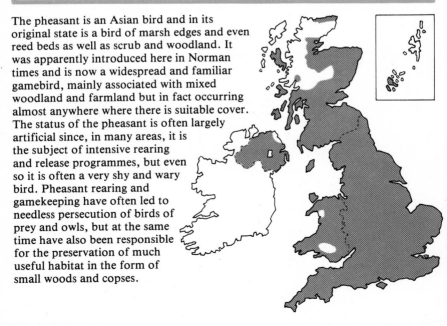

Woodcock

Scolopax rusticola

Size: 13½ in (34 cm).

Recognition: basically rufous-brown, paler below, beautifully marked with buff, brown and black.

Voice: in 'roding' flight males utter three low, grunting croaks followed by a high 'tsiwick'.

Nesting: a ground-nester. Normally 4 eggs, incubated by female for about 21 days; young leave nest soon after hatching.

Feeding: feeds in open, in search of worms, but also eats insects and their larvae and some vegetable matter.

The woodcock nests and roosts by day in woodland, where it is usually only seen when flushed – a thick-set, reddish-brown bird twisting away through the trees. It becomes most active from dusk onwards, when birds fly out to regular feeding areas. In the breeding season males are seen over woodland and around wood edges at dusk, flying with a curiously slow, deliberate action and uttering a series of low grunts and a more audible 'tsiwick' call: this is 'roding', not a territorial display flight as was once thought, but the male advertising himself as he searches for a mate. Woodcock are both residents and migrants, large numbers of birds coming into Britain from the Continent in winter. They are popular 'sporting birds' and are shot in large numbers.

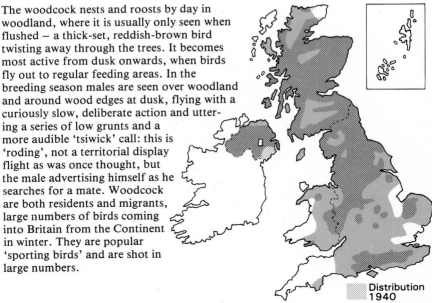

Distribution
1940

Stock Dove

Columba oenas

Size: 13 in (33 cm).

Recognition: smaller than woodpigeon and basically blue-grey, with black flight-feathers and tip to tail, vinous breast and iridescent green at sides of neck.

Voice: a low, double 'ooo-woo'.

Nesting: in woodland, nests in holes in trees, but elsewhere in cliffs and even rabbit burrows. Normally 2 eggs, incubated by both adults for 16 – 18 days, young fledging at about 4 weeks.

Feeding: seeds, cereals, leaves, roots, fruits, berries, nuts but also worms, insects and their larvae.

The stock dove has a wide distribution, but is nowhere as abundant as the woodpigeon. In woodland it is usually only found where there are old trees with holes suitable for nesting. It also occurs in open country and parkland with scattered trees and also along coastal cliffs and in quarries. In the early nineteenth century stock doves were more or less confined to southern and south-eastern England, but after that they expanded their range considerably, with the first breeding record for Ireland in 1866 and Scotland in 1877. Numbers declined again in the 1950s and early 1960s, probably due to the contamination of the birds' food supplies by toxic chemicals used in agriculture, but have increased again during the last 15 years as many of the more persistent chemicals have been withdrawn from use.

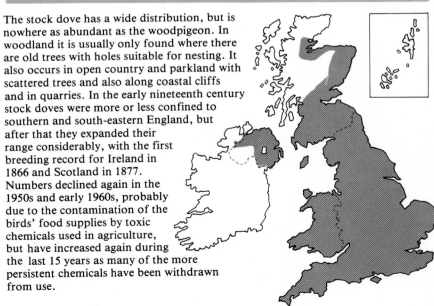

Woodpigeon

Columba palumbus

Size: 16 in (41 cm).

Recognition: largest pigeon, blue-grey above, vinous on breast, with conspicuous white neck-patch, white bar across wing and black-tipped tail.

Voice: a rhythmic 'coo-coo, coo-coo, coo'

Nesting: in woodland, also in hedgerows, and elsewhere in rock faces, on buildings or even on ground.

Feeding: much as stock dove. In winter often forms immense feeding flocks, not infrequently numbering in the thousands, foraging on farmland and roosting in nearby woodland.

Juv

Adult

The woodpigeon is one of the most familiar British birds, having spread even into the busiest towns and largest cities. It was originally a bird of deciduous woodland (in which, of course, it still occurs), but during the last two or three centuries has adapted to living in close association with arable farmland, nesting in copses, hedges and even single trees where woods are absent. During this century it has spread still further, reaching northernmost Scotland since the war and extending its range as far as Shetland and south-west Ireland. Huge numbers come into Britain from Europe in winter, joining the estimated 3 – 5 million pairs that breed here, and the damage caused by birds to growing crops is thought to be as high as £1 million per annum.

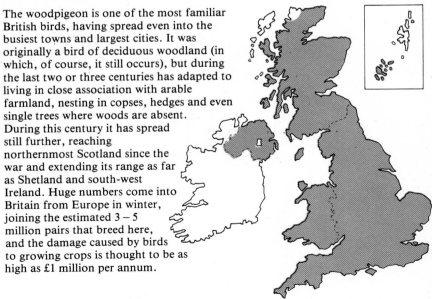

Turtle Dove

Streptopelia turtur

Size: 11 in (27 cm).

Recognition: small, slightly-built, chestnut on the back with black centres to the feathers, white tip to black tail, black-and-white neck-patch, pale vinous breast and white belly.

Voice: song is 'rroooorrrr, rroooorrrr, rroooorrrr'.

Nesting: nests in tall shrubs or small trees. Usually 2 eggs, incubated for about 14 days, the young leaving nest at 18 days and flying a few days later.

Feeding: mostly vegetable, but may also feed on a wide range of small invertebrates.

The turtle dove prefers fairly open woodland, or clearings in woods with large hawthorns and other bushes, but is also found in open country with scattered trees and mature hedgerows and in parks and large gardens. It is a summer visitor, arriving in late April and early May. It has increased and expanded its range in the wake of developing arable farming, but only just reaches Scotland (where it is a rare breeding bird) and has a very patchy distribution in the far west and in Ireland. Confusion often arises with the more familiar and widespread collared dove (a new colonist in Britain, unknown here before the 1950s), but that species is larger and generally paler, is seen here all through the year and is often closely associated with human habitations.

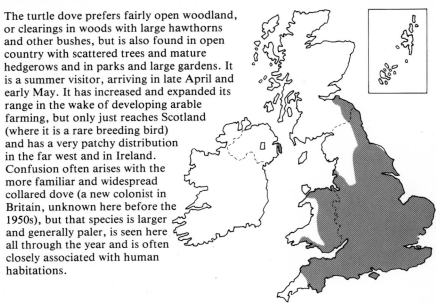

Tawny Owl

Strix aluco

Size: 15 in (38 cm).

Recognition: large head and broad rounded wings. Rufous-brown (rarely grey-brown) above, mottled and streaked darker, with white on scapulars and wing-coverts. Buffish below, heavily streaked with brown.

Voice: sharp 'kewick', with variants. Song is the familiar 'hooting'.

Nesting: nests in holes in trees. Usually 2 – 4 eggs, incubated by female for 28 – 30 days; young fly at 30 – 37 days.

Feeding: mainly small mammals in woodland.

The tawny owl, a stocky, medium-large bird, is thoroughly nocturnal, seldom abroad before dusk and roosting by day in hollow trees, in ivy or other cover, but sometimes in more open situations. It normally hunts from a perch, pouncing on to prey and killing with its talons or with a quick bite after capture. It is bold and aggressive, even towards man, in defence of its nest. Although essentially a woodland owl, it is highly adaptable and may occur anywhere with suitable trees – parkland, large gardens and all sorts of suburban areas, even right into large towns and cities where there are large squares and parks. It is by far the commonest British owl, but is absent from Ireland and most of the western and northern Scottish islands.

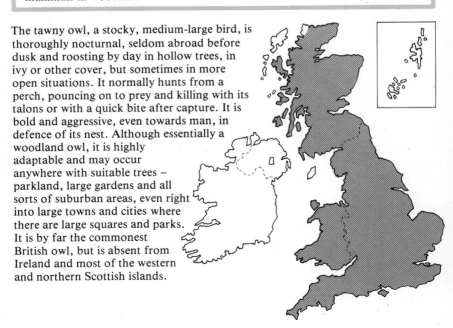

Long-eared Owl

Asio otus

Size: 14 in (36 cm).

Recognition: not unlike tawny owl, but smaller and slighter, rather greyer, with prominent erectile ear-like head-tufts and orange-yellow irises.

Voice: a low 'oo-oo-oo'. Characteristic 'unoiled hinge' call of young is often first indication of presence.

Nesting: usually uses old nest sometimes on ground. Usually 4 – 5 eggs, incubated by female for about 4 weeks, young leaving nest after about 23 days.

Feeding: hunts in open, as well as in woodland. Main prey: small mammals.

The long-eared owl is thoroughly nocturnal and, being much less vocal, is not as readily found as the tawny owl. Indeed, its distribution and numbers are only partly known over much of Britain. It favours mature coniferous woodland, including plantations, but is as much at home in mixed woodland or quite small copses, shelterbelts and thickets, and often nests where these adjoin extensive areas of open country where the bird usually hunts. In winter, traditional roost-sites are often used where small groups of owls may be found together, often in dense thickets and not necessarily near breeding areas. The head-tufts have nothing to do with hearing and are a means of visual communication between individual birds: the large ears are hidden in the feathers on the side of the head.

Nightjar

Caprimulgus europaeus

Size: 10¾ in (27 cm).

Recognition: grey-brown, beautifully marked with close pattern of brown and buff bars and speckles. Pointed wings, long tail, broad blunt head.

Voice: characteristic nasal 'gu-wick' in flight and song is a prolonged mechanical churring.

Nesting: nests on bare ground. Two eggs, incubated mainly by female for 18 days, young flying at 16 – 18 days.

Feeding: insects (especially night-flying moths).

The nightjar is only marginally a woodland bird – its preferred habitat being dry heathland. However, it is often associated with wood edges and broad woodland rides, where it often feeds, and in many areas has probably only maintained a presence in the face of habitat disappearance where commercial forestry occurs. Young plantations and wide firebreaks provide ideal nesting and feeding habitats. It nests among bark and other debris where the sitting female is perfectly camouflaged. Active only after dusk, nightjars can then be seen floating and gliding over open areas in search of insects, all of which are caught on the wing. It is a declining species, probably mainly due to little understood climatic factors, and over most of Britain and Ireland is very locally distributed.

Distribution 1958

Green Woodpecker

Picus viridis

Size: 12½ in (32 cm).

Recognition: easily identified by combination of dull green upperparts, with bright yellowish rump, paler underparts, red crown and black face and moustaches, the last with red centres in the male.

Voice: a loud ringing laugh or 'yaffle'.

Nesting: excavates hole in tree trunk. Usually 5 – 7 eggs, incubated for 15 – 17 days, the young flying at 18 – 21 days.

Feeding: in trees feeds on wood-boring insects and their larvae, but feeds often on the ground, breaking into ants' nests.

The green woodpecker is a bird of open deciduous woodland, especially with wide clearings and areas of short grass, but it is probably even more common in parkland, orchards, large gardens and other areas with widely scattered trees. Unlike the other British woodpeckers, it is not mainly arboreal and feeds on the ground, especially where ants are abundant. During the last 150 years it has spread northwards, with a particularly rapid colonisation of new areas over the last 35 years or so, so that it has now reached central and eastern Scotland and is still spreading northwards via the coastal lowlands. It is one of a number of birds whose populations are severely affected by hard winters and many local declines were reported following those of 1947, 1963 and 1979.

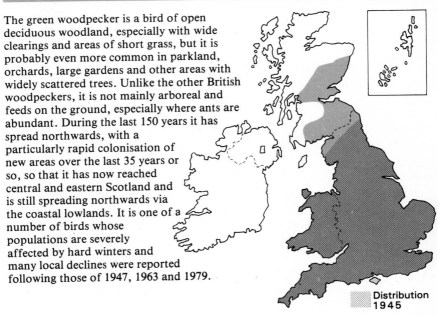

Distribution
1945

Great Spotted Woodpecker

Dendrocopus major

Size: 9 in (23 cm).

Recognition: thrush-sized, strikingly pied with red under-tail coverts; the male has a red spot at the nape. Fast, strongly undulating flight across open areas.

Voice: commonest note is a loud, sharp 'tchick'. Drums with bill on dead limbs, producing far-carrying sound of 8 – 10 blows.

Nesting: excavates hole in tree trunk. Usually 4 – 7 eggs, incubated for about 16 days, the young flying at 3 weeks.

Feeding: larvae of wood-boring insects, nuts, seeds, berries and nestling birds.

The great spotted woodpecker may occur virtually anywhere where there are trees, but it is much more closely associated with true woodland than the green woodpecker and is found in both deciduous and coniferous trees. Both species and the lesser spotted woodpecker are unknown as breeding birds in Ireland. It seems that the great spotted woodpecker vanished or became very scarce over much of northern England and almost all of Scotland in the nineteenth century, the reasons suggested for this including extensive felling and coppicing, competition with starlings for nest-sites and predation by red squirrels, but since the turn of the century the woodpecker has gradually recolonised much of its former range. Some birds occur here as winter visitors from northern Europe, occasionally arriving in quite considerable numbers.

Lesser Spotted Woodpecker

Dendrocopos minor

Size: 5¾ in (14.5 cm).

Recognition: a tiny, sparrow-sized woodpecker, white below and strongly barred black-and-white above, the male with red crown. Easily overlooked.

Voice: commonest note a high 'pee-pee-pee-pee-pee'. Drums like the great spotted woodpecker, but 10 – 30 blows, lasting 2 seconds and quieter.

Nesting: excavates hole in tree trunk or large limb. Usually 4 – 6 eggs, incubated for about 14 days, the young flying at 3 or 4 weeks.

Feeding: mainly arboreal insects and their larvae, but occasionally fruits and berries.

The lesser spotted woodpecker occurs in both deciduous and mixed woodland, but, like the green woodpecker and great spotted woodpecker, it may occur almost anywhere where there are trees, including orchards and gardens. It is often a somewhat retiring bird and can be difficult to find, even where it is tolerably common, even though it can be remarkably tame at times. In Britain it is essentially a southern species whose distribution seems to have changed little as far as we know, although temporary increases have occurred in some areas where the recent outbreaks of a particularly virulent form of Dutch elm disease have produced much dead wood and a large supply of suitable food. Recent records for Scotland (since 1966 – 67) are interesting in that they may indicate colonisation from northern Europe rather than England.

Jay

Garrulus glandarius

Size: 13½ in (34 cm).

Recognition: light brownish-pink, darker on the back, pale crown, striking black, white and blue wing-pattern and white rump contrasting with black tail.

Voice: usual note heard is a harsh 'skaaaak'.

Nesting: nests in thick cover in trees. Normally 5 – 6 eggs, incubated mainly by female for about 16 days, young flying at about 20 days.

Feeding: vegetable food, especially fruits and acorns ; also slugs, worms, insects, small mammals, young birds, eggs, etc.

Although occurring widely nowadays in parks and gardens in many areas, the jay is essentially a woodland bird, found in both broadleaved and coniferous woods, but often closely associated with oaks. Acorns form an important source of food in winter and, in autumn, jays are often seen foraging for them well away from their normal breeding areas; indeed, jays often bury acorns in 'food caches' and thus the bird indirectly helps the spread of oak woodland. The jay is one species which has benefited from the spread of new conifer woodlands in some areas. Today they are less heavily persecuted than they were a century ago, and have become more numerous as a result, but they are still regarded (probably unfairly) as 'vermin' and are shot in large numbers.

Great Tit

Parus major

Size: 5½ in (14 cm).

Recognition: largest tit, black head, striking white cheeks and black line down yellow underparts; juveniles much yellower than adults.

Voice: commonest calls are loud 'chink-chink-chink', sharp 'tui-tui-tui', 'see-see-see' and a scolding 'churr'.

Nesting: in holes, takes readily to nestboxes. Normally 5 – 11 eggs, incubated for 13 – 14 days, young flying at 18 – 20 days.

Feeding: insects and their larvae, spiders, worms, etc., fruits, seeds and buds.

Although best known to many as a bird of gardens, parks and orchards, and even as a 'town bird' in many areas, the great tit is a true woodland bird and one of a number which have adapted to live almost anywhere where there are trees or some cover. Its distribution covers almost all of mainland Britain and Ireland, though it is scarce in western Ireland, is rare in the Outer Hebrides and has only reached northernmost Scotland after a marked period of new colonisation during the last 50 years or so, no doubt helped by afforestation and a long series of milder winters. Our large resident population is augmented in autumn and win ter by the arrival of Continental great tits, which occasionally come in very considerable numbers, as happened in 1957.

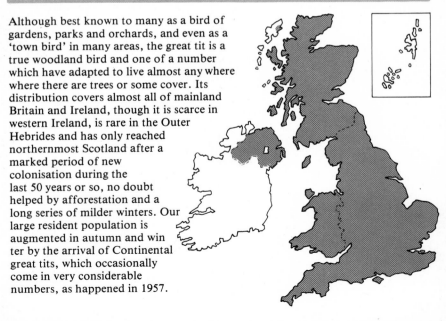

Blue Tit

Parus caeruleus

Size: 4½ in (11.5 cm).

Recognition: small, predominantly blue-and-yellow, with a bright blue crown and white cheeks; juveniles much yellower than adults.

Voice: commonest notes variations on 'tsee-tsee-tsee' and well-known scolding 'churr'.

Nesting: nests in holes in woodland chiefly in trees, or nestboxes where provided. Usually 7 – 14 eggs, incubated for 13 – 14 days, the young flying at about 19 days.

Feeding: mainly insects and their larvae, plus a wide range of fruits, grain, seeds, buds, etc.

To an even greater extent than the great tit, this species is very well known as a garden bird and may be found any place where there are trees or some other cover. In woodland, it is primarily a bird of deciduous trees, although it does occur in conifers and its spread in northernmost Scotland has been assisted by increasing numbers of new plantations. Interestingly, while its numbers have remained more or less static in woodland over the last 15 years or so, numbers on farmland and in other habitats have increased, helped no doubt in many suburban areas by the provision of nestboxes. Blue tits also occur here as winter visitors, occasionally in very considerable numbers, and huge numbers arrived here, along with great tits, in the famous 'irruption' of 1957.

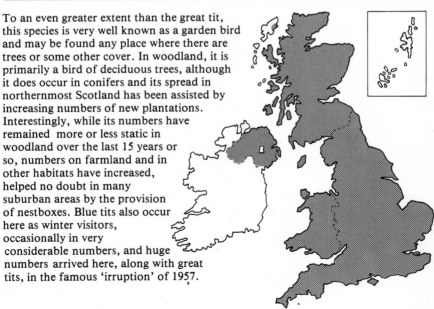

Coal Tit

Parus ater

Size: 4½ in (11.5 cm).

Recognition: a small tit, grey-brown above and buffish-white below, with more black on throat than the marsh or willow tit and a distinct white panel on the black nape.

Voice: a thin 'tsee-tsee-tsee' and loud piping 'tsiu' and similar notes. Song is clear, high 'peetoo, peetoo, peetoo'.

Nesting: nests in holes, usually in or near ground, often in bank or low stump or among tree roots. Usually 7 – 11 eggs, incubated for 17 – 18 days, young flying at about 16 days.

Food: mainly insects, larvae and spiders, also some seeds.

Adult

Juv

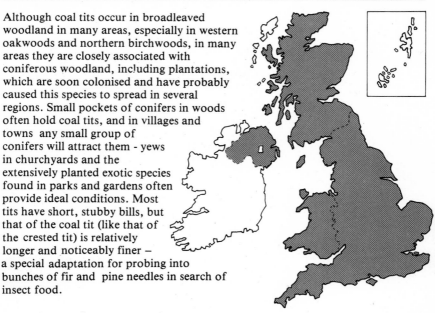

Although coal tits occur in broadleaved woodland in many areas, especially in western oakwoods and northern birchwoods, in many areas they are closely associated with coniferous woodland, including plantations, which are soon colonised and have probably caused this species to spread in several regions. Small pockets of conifers in woods often hold coal tits, and in villages and towns any small group of conifers will attract them - yews in churchyards and the extensively planted exotic species found in parks and gardens often provide ideal conditions. Most tits have short, stubby bills, but that of the coal tit (like that of the crested tit) is relatively longer and noticeably finer – a special adaptation for probing into bunches of fir and pine needles in search of insect food.

Crested Tit

Parus cristatus

Size: 4½ (11.5 cm).

Recognition: basically brown above and white below, distinct black-and-white face, prominent pointed crest, whitish with black markings.

Voice: most characteristic call is a curious, relatively low-pitched trill — quite unlike the call of any other British tit.

Nesting: excavates hole in rotten pine stump, sometimes in birch or post, only rarely using natural hole.

Feeding: insects and larvae, plus some seeds, etc. Like coal tit, has relatively fine bill for feeding among pine needles.

On the Continent the crested tit is a widely distributed bird, occurring in both conifers and mixed woodland, but in Britain it is confined to a small part of Scotland, its relict distribution being closely associated with the remnants of the old Caledonian Pine Forest. Presumably it was much more numerous centuries ago when much greater areas of this semi-open forest existed, with its old trees, decaying wood and extensive ground-cover of heather, bilberry and juniper. In recent years there has been a gradual and interesting spread of crested tits into some of the more extensive and mature coniferous plantations, helped in some areas by the provision of nestboxes. These Scottish and Continental birds are largely sedentary, so it is unlikely that the many possibly suitable areas in England and Wales will ever be colonised.

Marsh Tit

Parus palustris

Size: 4½ in (11.5 cm).

Recognition: plain brown above, whitish below, with white cheeks, small black bib and glossy black crown. *See also* willow tit.

Voice: characteristic note is distinctive 'pitchew', with variations. *See also* willow tit.

Nesting: nests in natural holes in trees, stumps, etc., occasionally in nestboxes. Usually 7 – 8 eggs, incubated for about 13 days, young flying at about 16 – 17 days.

Feeding: mainly insects and their larvae.

Marsh and willow tits are confusingly alike – *see* willow tit for identification details. The willow tit was not separated from the marsh tit by observers in Britain until 1900, so most of the early history of the two species' distribution remains obscure. Marsh tits have a basically southern distribution, only just extending into south-east Scotland and not reaching far into north-western England. Willow tits occur slightly further north, especially in the west, but have apparently declined markedly in the Highlands over the last 50 to 60 years. Marsh tits are quite wrongly named, being mainly birds of deciduous woodland with no particular liking for wet places; if anything, wetter woodland and carr is more favoured by the willow tit, which normally likes rotting wood in which to excavate its nest-hole.

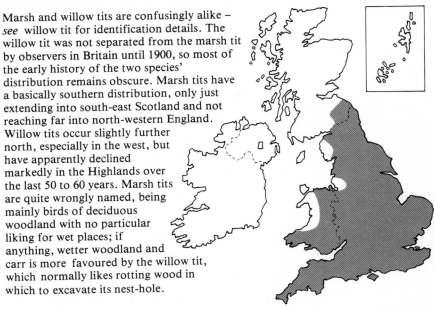

Willow Tit

Parus montanus

Size: 4½ in (11.5 cm).

Recognition: plain brown above, usually with a noticeable pale panel on the closed wing, whitish below, white cheeks, small black bib and dull black cap.

Voice: thin, high 'zee-zee-zee' and variants; a nasal, slurred, buzzing 'zurr-zurr-zurr-zurr' is diagnostic.

Nesting: excavates nest-hole. Usually 8 – 9 eggs, incubated for about 13 – 14 days, the young flying after 17 – 19 days.

Feeding: basically very similar to that of marsh tit.

With much field experience of both species, it is possible to tell marsh and willow tits apart by the relative shapes of their black bibs and crowns and the amount of white on the cheeks. Also in the best light conditions the crown of the marsh tit is glossy, while that of the willow tit is dull. Most willow tits also show a strikingly pale panel along the closed wing, which is absent in typical marsh tits. However, none of these characteristics is 100 per cent reliable and voice (or a combination of voice and the above features) is usually the safest means of identification. The songs are quite different, but the best distinctions are the low, buzzing 'zurr-zurr-zurr-zurr' of the willow and the loud 'pitchew' calls of the marsh.

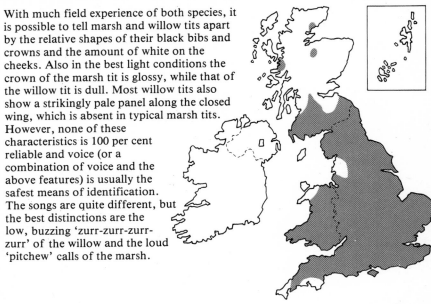

Long-tailed Tit

Aegithalos caudatus

Size: 5½ in (14 cm).

Recognition: a tiny, long-tailed bird, unmistakable with its unique combination of white, pink and black plumage.

Voice: quiet, abrupt 'tupp' or a very characteristic slurred 'sirrupp', and a high, thin 'see-see-see', all on one note.

Nesting: nest is egg-shaped with hole in side, of mosses, cobwebs, lichens, etc., lined with masses of feathers. Usually 8 – 12 eggs, incubated for 14 – 18 days, the young flying at 15 – 16 days.

Feeding: mainly insects and larvae.

In body size, the long-tailed tit is a tiny bird, a considerable part of its quoted size being its very long tail. It is a familiar bird in most types of woodland, but is probably more generally associated with a very wide range of other habitats wherever trees and bushes occur. In autumn and winter it is often encountered in small flocks, or family parties, and often associates with flocks of other tits, treecreepers and goldcrests. Even so, it is probably not very closely related to the other tits, which differ most markedly in being hole-nesting birds. It is widely distributed and generally fairly common (often occurring in gardens and parks in many areas) and its distribution has changed little this century, though it is particularly susceptible to very hard winters.

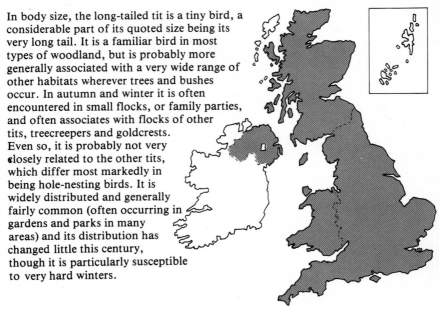

Nuthatch

Sitta europaea

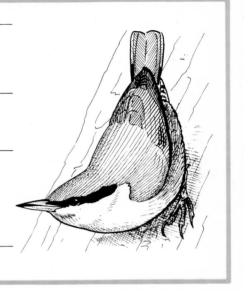

Size: 5½ in (14 cm).

Recognition: dumpy, big-headed, short-tailed, basically grey-blue above with a black eyestripe, buffish underparts and chestnut on the flanks.

Voice: a loud, ringing 'chwit, chwit,'chwit', and piping song based on 'twee', 'pee' or 'chew' notes.

Nesting: nests in natural holes in trees and in nestboxes, plastering the hole with mud until aperture size is correct. Normally 6 – 11 eggs, incubated for about 15 days, the young flying at 23 – 25 days.

Feeding: a wide range of insect food, nuts, seeds, etc.

The nuthatch is a very noisy and distinctive bird. It clambers about trees with quite amazing dexterity, often moving crosswise on trunks or along the underside of horizontal limbs and even descending trunks headfirst – something which woodpeckers and treecreepers cannot do. It feeds just as readily on the ground, and wedges nuts, seeds, etc. in cracks in bark, cracking them open with heavy blows from its bill. Its distribution, which is mainly in the southern half of mainland Britain, is curiously patchy; even though their preferred habitats of old deciduous woodland and open parkland, especially with oaks, beeches and chestnuts, may be present, nuthatches may not! Large parks, even in towns, and gardens with mature trees also attract them and they will come readily to bird tables and often use nestboxes if provided.

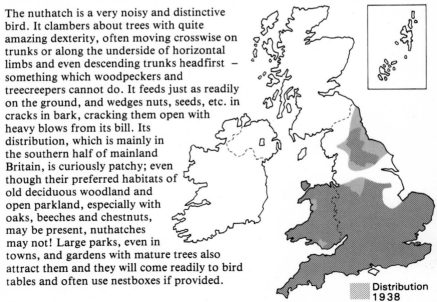

Distribution 1938

Treecreeper

Certhia familiaris

Size: 5 in (12.5 cm).

Recognition: small, easily overlooked brown bird, streaked darker above, with a whitish stripe over the eye and whitish wingbars, and white below.

Voice: an insistent, high-pitched 'seee seee seee', the notes often widely spaced, is call most commonly heard; high pitched song 'tee-tee-tee-titidooee' is very distinctive.

Nesting: nests in cracks, crevices or large splits in tree trunks. Usually 6 eggs, incubated for 17 – 20 days, young flying at 14 – 15 days.

Feeding: chiefly insects.

Treecreepers are more often heard than seen, but they are often fairly tame and will permit observation at close quarters as they climb jerkily up tree trunks and along larger limbs, often working from one side of the tree to the other and then flying down to the base of another tree to begin again. In winter they are often found in company with tits and goldcrests in mixed, roving flocks and at this season they may also roost in shallow depressions which they excavate in the soft bark of Wellingtonias. Their distribution and range has apparently changed little since ornithological recording began: they are widespread in deciduous and mixed woodlands and are often found in conifers. Indeed they may occur almost anywhere with suitable trees, including in gardens.

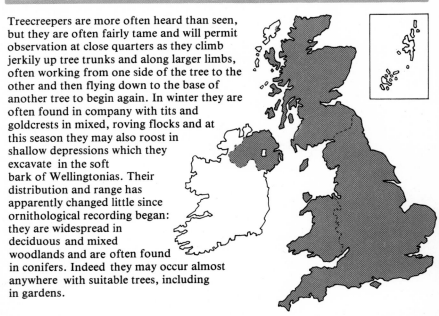

Wren

Troglodytes troglodytes

Size: 3½ in (9.5 cm).

Recognition: a tiny, dumpy bird with a very short tail, usually held cocked up, rich brown above and paler below, with buffish eyestripe.

Voice: song is incredibly loud for the size of the bird — a long, rattling series of trills and warbles ending with a flourish. Commonest call is a hard 'tic-tic-tic'.

Nesting: builds a large, domed nest with entrance hole in side. Usually 5 – 6 eggs, incubated for about 14 – 15 days, the young flying at about 16 – 17 days.

Feeding: insects.

The wren is one of the most abundant and widespread of British birds: before the hard winter of 1979 reduced numbers dramatically (wrens are always notoriously susceptible to severe winters) there may have been some 10 million pairs in Britain and Ireland. It is also one of the most versatile and adaptable, being found in almost every imaginable kind of habitat and even occurring on remote islands such as those of the St Kilda group. It is therefore just as much a bird of sea cliffs, mountain country and heathland as it is of all kinds of woodland, although it is probably most numerous where trees and scrub occur. It is also worth mentioning that wrens are New World birds which have colonised the Old World: they probably reached the British Isles over 7000 years ago.

Song Thrush

Turdus philomelos

Size: 9 in (23 cm).

Recognition: plain warm brown above, buff on breast with regular pattern of close dark spots. The mistle thrush is much larger, greyer brown, with larger, more irregularly spaced spots below and white tips to outer tail-feathers (see drawing).

Voice: main call a short 'tsip'; song is loud and ringing.

Nesting: usually in low bushes or trees. Normally 4 – 5 eggs, incubated for 13 – 14 days, young fledging at 13 – 14 days.

Feeding: mainly worms and molluscs.

Mistle thrush

Song thrush

The song thrush is another highly adaptable and familiar bird, often seen in parks and gardens, and well known both for its remarkable song and its habit of using stones as 'anvils' on which it breaks open snail shells. It occurs in virtually all types of woodland, and indeed almost anywhere where there is some cover, but like the blackbird it is not an abundant bird in high forest. To a much greater extent than is generally realised, song thrushes often suffer badly in prolonged hard weather and their numbers declined considerably after the severe winters of 1947 and 1963, and probably also in that of 1979: recovery, however, is generally fairly rapid in intervening series of milder winters. Large numbers of Continental song thrushes migrate through Britain in autumn and to some extent winter with us.

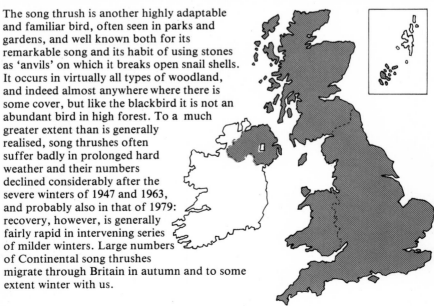

Blackbird

Turdus merula

Size: 10 in (25 cm).

Recognition: male is wholly black with yellow bill and eye-ring. Female dark brown, lighter below with dark streaks from throat.

Voice: rich, languid, fluty song well known. Loud rattle of alarm when disturbed.

Nesting: usually nests in low bushes, small trees, ivy, etc. Normally 4 – 5 eggs, incubated for 13 – 14 days, young fledging at 13 – 14 days.

Feeding: wide range of fruits, berries and seeds; also worms, insects and their larvae, spiders, molluscs, etc.

♀

Because it is one of our commonest birds and is so well known as a bird of gardens and town parks, the blackbird needs little introduction. It is in fact found in a very wide range of habitats, almost anywhere where there is some cover, and may occur in virtually any kind of woodland, although it is perhaps more a bird of wood edges and open woodland with glades and rides than of high forest. It is absent only from the highest and barest areas, but during this century has extended its range northwards and westwards on to the outermost and northernmost Scottish islands and westwards in Ireland. Its mountain counterpart, the ring ouzel, has declined in many areas, perhaps partly as a result of increasing competition from colonising blackbirds.

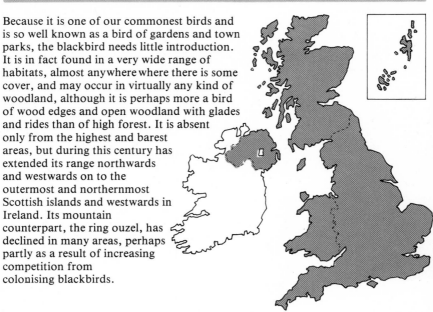

Redstart

Phoenicurus phoenicurus

Size: 5½ in (14 cm).

Recognition: male blue-grey above, with white forehead, black face and throat, orange-red breast and tail; female light brown above, buffish below, also with red tail.

Voice: main calls: a loud 'hooeet' and a characteristic 'weet-tuc-tuc'. Song is a brief jingle ending in a trill.

Nesting: a hole-nester, taking readily to nestboxes. Usually 5 – 6 eggs, incubated for 12 – 14 days, the young flying at about 2 weeks.

Feeding: principally insects, also spiders, worms and some berries, etc.

♂ Summer

♂ Autumn

♀

Redstarts are found in a variety of woodland habitats, but tend perhaps to prefer open or semi-open mature woodland and wood edges; they also occur quite widely in parkland, along old hedgerows with mature trees, in orchards and in large gardens. They are reasonably well distributed over the greater part of Britain wherever suitable habitat exists, but are rare in Ireland and are curiously scarce in many parts of eastern England. Redstart numbers have declined noticeably in Britain during the past decade: like some other birds which are summer visitors to Britain, they have major winter quarters along the Sahel zone on the southern fringes of the Sahara. Extreme drought conditions there over a number of years have brought famine to humans and livestock and high mortality to many small birds.

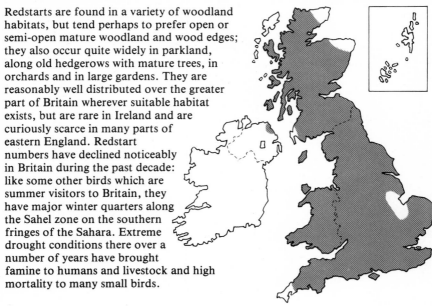

Nightingale

Luscinia megarhynchos

Size: 6½ in (16.5 cm).

Recognition: warm brown above, with a russet tail, pale greyish-brown underparts. Usually a furtive bird.

Voice: various grating alarm calls, a hard 'tuc, tuc' and a soft 'hweet'. Remarkable song is rich, varied, vigorous and often loud, with incredibly quick phrasing.

Nesting: nests in thick cover. Usually 4 – 5 eggs, incubated for 13 – 14 days, the young flying at about 12 days.

Feeding: chiefly insects, larvae and worms, but also spiders and some fruits and berries.

The nightingale is a summer migrant, famed for its song. Contrary to popular belief, it sings during the day, but song is most frequent from dusk into the early part of the night and again before dawn, its voice often (but not always) being the only one to be heard after dark. Nightingales are birds of thicketed commons and dense scrub, and in woodland favour areas of coppice-with-standards which produce the right mosaic of undergrowth and open areas. Coppicing as a method of woodland management is in decline: neglected coppiced woodland eventually becomes too dark and overgrown for nightingales and it is this neglect which has led to a gradual decrease in the numbers of birds in many areas of woodland. Scrub clearance has also taken a fair toll.

Distribution 1910

Robin

Erithacus rubecula

Size: 5½ in (14 cm).

Recognition: olive-brown above, orange-red forehead, face and breast, bordered with pale blue-grey; juvenile lacks the 'red breast' and is conspicuously spotted.

Voice: main calls 'tic, tic, tic', 'seee'. Song a sweet varied warble.

Nesting: nests in low cover, but will use all sorts of 'artificial' sites. Usually 4 – 6 eggs, incubated for 13 – 14 days, the young flying at 12 – 14 days.

Feeding: mainly insects and larvae, spiders, centipedes, assorted fruits, berries.

The robin, Britain's 'national bird', is so well known as a perky, trusting bird of parks and gardens that its origins as a bird of deciduous high forest are often forgotten. It has adapted to a wide range of conditions, both inside and outside woodland, and is today one of the commonest and most widely distributed of all British birds. Its distribution is almost total, with only the highest and barest areas and the outermost and northernmost islands totally or partially excluded. Numbers and distribution have remained virtually unaltered since the second half of the last century, but the species may suffer local declines as a result of hard winters. Robins are resident birds, but many Continental migrants pass through in autumn and some remain with us as winter visitors.

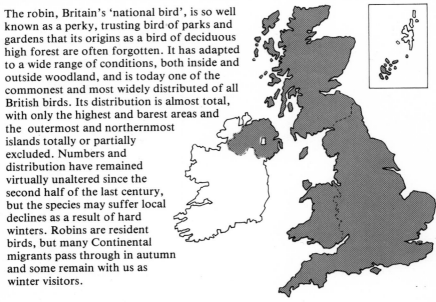

Blackcap

Sylvia atricapilla

Size: 5½ in (14 cm).

Recognition: greyish-brown above, male ashy-grey below, female somewhat browner below. Cap black in male, reddish-brown in female.

Voice: sharp, scolding 'tac, tac' and a short 'churrr'. Clear, rich, warbling song.

Nesting: nests in bushes, briars, etc. Normally 5 eggs, incubated for 10 – 11 days, the young fledging at about 10 – 13 days.

Feeding: mainly insects, taken while foraging in bushes and trees, seldom from ground, and fruits and berries, especially in autumn.

The majority of blackcaps are summer migrants, although in recent years they have shown an increasing tendency to overwinter with us, often being first detected when they visit garden feeding stations. Blackcaps occur in mature deciduous woodland and in mixed woodland, usually where there is a good shrub layer, but are also found in thick scrub, coppices, large gardens and the edges of conifer plantations. Their association with rhododendrons, especially in Ireland and parts of Scotland, is probably largely accidental, since this introduced shrub occurs widely in large estates and parks which often also contain the best deciduous woodland for blackcaps. Garden warblers and blackcaps often occur together and their range and choice of habitat are roughly the same: how two, apparently similar species co-exist without competition is little understood.

Garden Warbler

Sylvia borin

Size: 5½ in (14 cm).

Recognition: a singularly plain bird with no real distinguishing features, apart from rather compact build, rounded head and short bill. Brownish above, pale buffish below.

Voice: song is very similar to blackcap's, but is generally longer, slightly lower in pitch and with more hurried phrases.

Nesting: nests in cover. Normally 4 – 5 eggs, incubated for about 12 days, the young flying at 9 – 10 days.

Feeding: mainly insects, but also spiders and small worms.

The rather similar songs of garden warblers and blackcaps can confuse even the most experienced birdwatchers at times – many like to clinch identification by actually seeing the singer. Garden warblers are easily told from other warblers by the rather negative fact that they are totally 'plain' in appearance – other warblers usually have eyestripes or wingbars, or some other relieving feature. They occur in much the same sort of habitats as blackcaps, but are perhaps found more often away from mature trees in scrub and even young plantations. Both blackcaps and garden warblers seem to have remained fairly stable in terms of range and numbers for as long as ornithologists have kept records; both become scarcer and more scattered north of the Scottish Lowlands, and garden warblers are noticeably scarcer in Ireland.

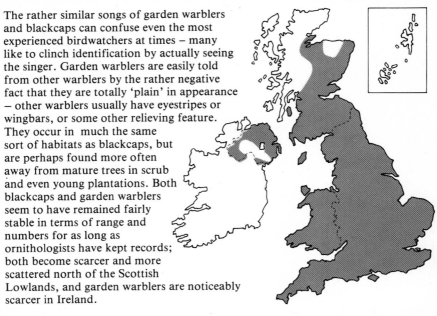

Willow Warbler

Phylloscopus trochilus

Size: 4¼ in (11 cm).

Recognition: a small warbler, olive-brown and pale below, underparts with yellowish wash. Legs usually pinkish-brown.

Voice: normal call note is a clear, disyllabic 'hooeet'. Song a musical descending cadence, ending with a short flourish.

Nesting: normally nests on ground, in grass or other low vegetation. Usually 6 – 7 eggs, incubated by female for about 13 days. Young fledge after about 14 days.

Feeding: feeds on small insects, larvae and small worms.

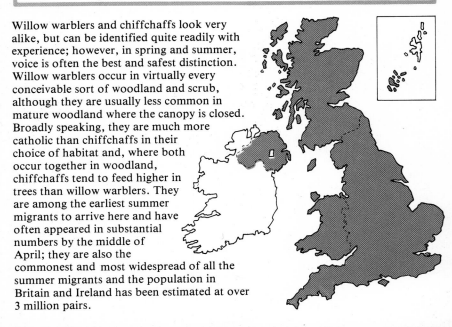

Willow warblers and chiffchaffs look very alike, but can be identified quite readily with experience; however, in spring and summer, voice is often the best and safest distinction. Willow warblers occur in virtually every conceivable sort of woodland and scrub, although they are usually less common in mature woodland where the canopy is closed. Broadly speaking, they are much more catholic than chiffchaffs in their choice of habitat and, where both occur together in woodland, chiffchaffs tend to feed higher in trees than willow warblers. They are among the earliest summer migrants to arrive here and have often appeared in substantial numbers by the middle of April; they are also the commonest and most widespread of all the summer migrants and the population in Britain and Ireland has been estimated at over 3 million pairs.

Chiffchaff

Phylloscopus collybita

Size: 4¼ in (11 cm).

Recognition: closely resembles willow warbler, but normally rather browner above and less yellowish below; the legs are usually dark - but some willow warblers may also have dark legs.

Voice: commonest call 'hweet' – more monosyllabic than similar call of willow warbler. Song is best identification feature – repeated 'chiff-chaff', etc.

Nesting: nests in cover on or near ground. Normally 6 eggs, incubated for about 13 days, the young flying at 14 days.

Feeding: mainly small insects.

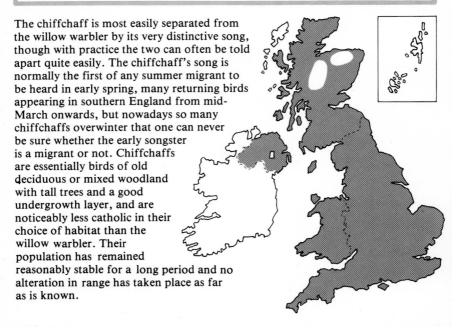

The chiffchaff is most easily separated from the willow warbler by its very distinctive song, though with practice the two can often be told apart quite easily. The chiffchaff's song is normally the first of any summer migrant to be heard in early spring, many returning birds appearing in southern England from mid-March onwards, but nowadays so many chiffchaffs overwinter that one can never be sure whether the early songster is a migrant or not. Chiffchaffs are essentially birds of old deciduous or mixed woodland with tall trees and a good undergrowth layer, and are noticeably less catholic in their choice of habitat than the willow warbler. Their population has remained reasonably stable for a long period and no alteration in range has taken place as far as is known.

Wood Warbler

Phylloscopus sibilatrix

Size: 5 in (12.5 cm).

Recognition: larger than chiff-chaff or willow warbler with longer wings and shorter tail; brighter green above, with yellow eyestripe, yellow breast contrasting with white belly.

Voice: normal call a piping 'puu', which forms basis of one of the two forms of song —'puu, puu, puu, puu'; other song phase a high shivering trill on one note.

Nesting: nests on ground in undergrowth. Normally 6 – 7 eggs, incubated for about 13 days, the young flying at 11 – 12 days.

Feeding: mainly insects.

The wood warbler spends much of its time high in the treetops, where its characteristic shape, often with the wings drooped, and its active pursuit of insects among the leaves and into the air are very distinctive. In Britain, it is closely tied to mature woodland with little or no ground cover, being a much more arboreal bird than either the chiffchaff or the willow warbler. Basically its distribution closely follows that of the western and northern sessile oakwoods, but in southern and eastern England it occurs in beech, chestnut and oak; further north it is often found in birchwoods. There has been a gradual decrease in many eastern areas but, on the other hand, the wood warbler has been slowly extending its range northwards in Scotland since the middle of the nineteenth century.

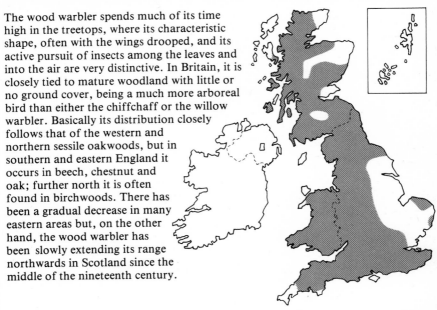

Goldcrest

Regulus regulus

Size: 3½ in (9 cm).

Recognition: a tiny, rather short-tailed bird, greenish above and a dingy white below, with a double wingbar and a yellowish crest bordered with black *(see below)*.

Voice: very high, thin 'zeee-zeee-zeee' calls, song a high 'seeta-seeta-seeta-seeta-sissi-pee.

Nesting: suspends nest under foliage. Usually 7 – 10 eggs, incubated for 14 – 16 days, young flying at about 3 weeks.

Feeding: mainly small insects and their larvae and spiders.

Juv

Adult

Most bird books show the female's crest as yellow and that of the male as yellow with a bright orange centre; these details are correct, but in practice it is usually exceptionally difficult to see them in the field – goldcrests of either sex almost always appear to have indistinguishable yellow crowns. They are essentially birds of coniferous woodland (including plantations), but, like the coal tit, they may be found in church-yards, gardens and parks wherever pockets of conifers, including exotic species, occur. To a lesser extent, they also live in mixed and deciduous woodland (more often perhaps in winter), especially when populations are high after long runs of mild winters, but are quite numerous in sessile oakwoods in Ireland.

The spread of commercial conifer plantations has undoubtedly benefited this species.

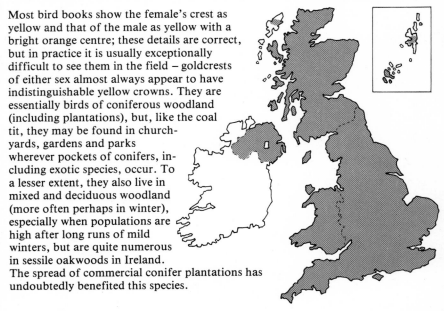

Firecrest

Regulus ignicapillus

Size: 3½ in (9 cm).

Recognition: very like goldcrest, but brighter green above and whiter below; bronze patch at shoulder visible in good light; head quite different: black stripe through eye, whitish stripe above and some white below. More orange-red in crest, especially male.

Voice: similar to goldcrest, but generally lower-pitched and louder. Distinctive trilling song, lacking flourish at end.

Nesting: breeding cycle is broadly similar to goldcrest.

Feeding: small insects and spiders.

For a long time the firecrest was regarded as a passage migrant and winter visitor, mainly to the southern half of Britain, but following an expansion of range on the Continent it has now established itself here as a breeding species. Nesting was suspected in the New Forest in 1961 and confirmed in 1962, and now it is known to nest in a number of scattered localities in southern England. It is easily overlooked and may well be breeding in other areas. Firecrests are not as closely tied to conifers as goldcrests, but those nesting in England appear to have particularly favoured fairly mature Norway spruce, although others have set up home in other conifers, in mixed woods and even in oak and beech with a good mixture of holly.

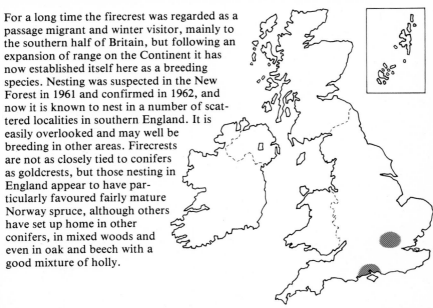

Spotted Flycatcher

Muscicapa striata

Size: 5½ in (14 cm).

Recognition: a grey-brown bird, with pale underparts, small dark spots and streaks on the crown and dark streaking down the breast. Juveniles are noticeably spotted paler.

Voice: a shrill 'tzeee', a short 'tchik' and, when alarmed, 'zeec-tzuc'.

Nesting: usually nests against tree trunk or wall, or on branch, beam, etc., occasionally in hole. Normally 4 – 5 eggs incubated for 12 – 14 days, the young flying at 12 – 13 days.

Feeding: almost entirely insects.

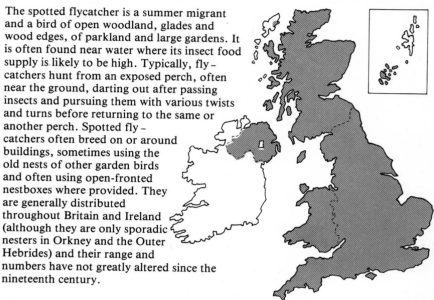

The spotted flycatcher is a summer migrant and a bird of open woodland, glades and wood edges, of parkland and large gardens. It is often found near water where its insect food supply is likely to be high. Typically, flycatchers hunt from an exposed perch, often near the ground, darting out after passing insects and pursuing them with various twists and turns before returning to the same or another perch. Spotted flycatchers often breed on or around buildings, sometimes using the old nests of other garden birds and often using open-fronted nestboxes where provided. They are generally distributed throughout Britain and Ireland (although they are only sporadic nesters in Orkney and the Outer Hebrides) and their range and numbers have not greatly altered since the nineteenth century.

Pied Flycatcher

Ficedula hypoleucos

Size: 5 in (13 cm).

Recognition: summer male unmistakable – black above with white on forehead, white wingbar and white underparts. Female grey-brown above, whitish below, whitish wingbar.

Voice: a sharp 'whit' and 'tic tic'; alarm call 'hweet'.

Nesting: nests in natural holes in trees, also old walls, buildings, etc., and takes very readily to nestboxes. Usually 5 – 9 eggs, incubated for 12 – 13 days, the young fledging at about 13 – 14 days.

Feeding: mainly insects, also caterpillars, etc.

Pied flycatchers are summer migrants, breeding almost completely in deciduous woodland in hill valleys or alongside rivers and lakes. Their distribution approximates quite closely to that of the western sessile oakwoods, always a preferred habitat. To some extent their distribution is governed by the availability of old timber with holes suitable for nesting, but the provision of nestboxes soon enables them to increase their numbers in some areas and to colonise new ones. The bird's range expanded quite considerably during 1941 – 52, and, although there has been little overall change in the last 25 years, a slow move northwards has continued. Pied flycatchers apparently bred quite often in parts of eastern England a century ago, but they are almost unknown there today, except as numerous passage migrants, especially in autumn.

Distribution
1938

Dunnock

Prunella modularis

Size: 5¾ in (14.5 cm).

Recognition: superficially sparrow-like, but fine bill, grey head with browner ear-coverts, grey underparts, streaked flanks and warm brown upperparts, streaked darker.

Voice: usual call a loud, rather shrill 'tseep' singly or in series; song is pleasant, musical, high-pitched warbling.

Nesting: nests in cover near ground. Usually 4 – 5 eggs, incubated for 12 – 13 days, young flying at about 12 days.

Feeding: mainly animal food in summer turning more to vegetable food in winter. Comes readily to garden feeding stations, though seldom seen on bird tables.

Dunnocks are often called 'hedge sparrows', but in reality they are not sparrows at all and belong to the accentor family. In Britain they are birds of open or semi-open woodland, often where there is associated scrub or good secondary growth of brambles, briars, etc., and of hedgerows, commons, parks and gardens. In the Hebrides they are often birds of open country with gorse, heather and bracken. In a woodland context they are interesting as one of the first birds to colonise new scrub and newly-developing woodlands, including new conifer plantations while the trees are small and the plantation retains an open aspect Dunnocks are both widespread and common throughout Britain and Ireland and their status has probably not changed much in historic times, apart from a slight northward spread in Scotland.

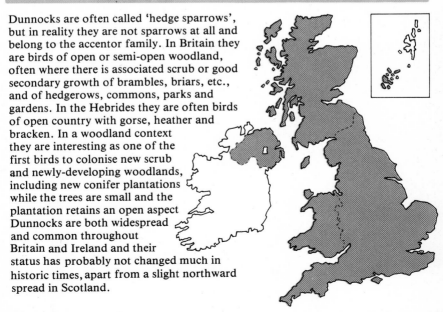

Tree Pipit

Anthus trivialis

Size: 6 in (15 cm).

Recognition: brown, streaked darker above, yellowish-buff on the breast with fine dark streaks. Flesh-coloured legs, white outer tail-feathers.

Voice: voice is often best distinction from meadow pipit: call is a curiously rasping 'teez'. Full song is diagnostic, finishing with loud 'seeeaa, seeeaa, seeeaa'.

Nesting: nests on ground; usually 4 – 6 eggs, incubated for about 14 days, young flying at about 12 – 13 days.

Feeding: mainly insects and their larvae, spiders, etc.

Most pipits are birds of true open country, but the tree pipit is found in areas of open woodland where there are large clearings, glades and rides, around wood edges and in places where there are scattered trees or tall bushes: a combination of prominent song-perches (from where they launch their characteristic 'parachuting' song-flight) and open grassy areas for feeding is essential tree-pipit habitat. New conifer plantations are ideal for this species, at least for a short period, and they are among the first colonists of this 'new woodland' During the last 100 years, tree pipits have spread northwards in Scotland: they are now typical birds in many northern birchwoods and open pine forest. Some local fluctuations have occurred in southern England and the bird has disappeared here and there, partly at least due to loss of habitat.

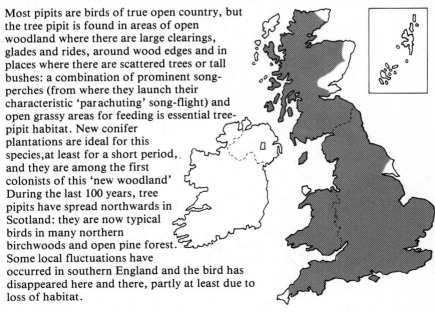

Starling

Sturnus vulgaris

Size: 8½ in (21.5 cm).

Recognition: basically blackish, with green and purple iridescences, liberally spotted; more markedly spotted white in winter, especially below.

Voice: an almost unbelievable range of calls; strongly mimetic, especially in long, rambling song.

Nesting: nests mainly in holes. Usually 5 – 7 eggs, incubated for 12 – 13 days, the young flying at about 3 weeks.

Feeding: a wide range of insects, larvae, worms, especially in summer, fruits, seed, berries and so forth.

Juv

The starling is too well known a bird of gardens, parks and urban situations to need much description. In fact it is one of the most catholic of all birds in its choice of habitats, occurring virtually everywhere except on the highest and most remote uplands, and forming large flocks (often immense at roosts) in winter, when the estimated 4 – 7 million pairs in Britain and Ireland are joined by huge numbers of European birds, some from as far away as Russia. Starlings declined over much of Britain in the early nineteenth century, virtually disappearing from most of mainland Scotland and Ireland and from west Wales and south-west England, but during the last 150 years they have spread back again, mainly as a result of climate amelioration.

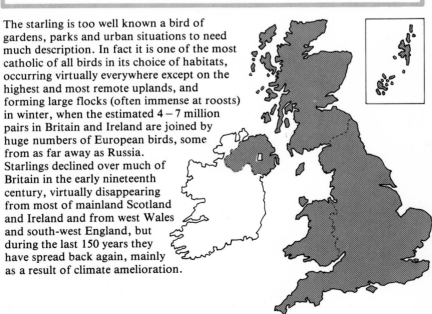

Hawfinch

Coccothraustes coccothraustes

Size: 7 in (18 cm).

Recognition: dumpy and short-tailed, with big head and outsize stout bill. Brown on back, black chin, grey nape, large white wing-patch most obvious in flight, white tip to black tail.

Voice: main call, is a sharp 'tzick' or 'tzick-tzick' – often the first indication of this elusive bird's presence.

Nesting: nests in trees or large bushes. Usually 4 – 6 eggs, incubated for about 9 – 10 days, young fledging at 10 – 11 days.

Feeding: mainly seeds and kernels, also beechmast.

This extraordinary bird is one of the most difficult of woodland birds to get to know: although hawfinches on the Continent are often obvious and even quite tame, here they are usually extremely shy and wary and are probably more often heard than seen. They are birds of deciduous woodland, especially where trees with large fruits are present – they have a particular liking for hornbeam, beech and wild cherry, for example. Large gardens with fruit trees and orchards are also good hawfinch habitat. The huge bill enables them to crack open large seeds, even cherry stones, to get at the kernels. Little is known for certain about the history of their scattered distribution, or whether it has changed much in the last 150 years. They are commonest in south-east England.

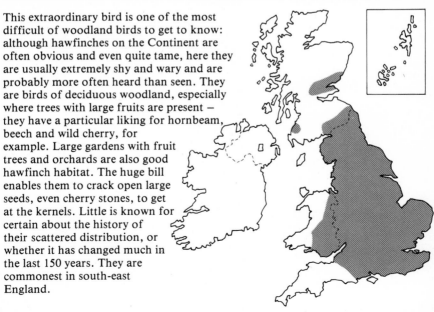

Greenfinch

Carduelis chloris

Size: 5¾ in (14.5 cm).

Recognition: male olive-green, yellower on rump, conspicuous yellow markings on wings and tail. Pale, rather heavy bill. Female duller with less yellow.

Voice: loud, liquid trilling and a nasal 'sweeer'. Song is mixture of calls and prolonged twittering.

Nesting: nests in bushes, evergreens, small trees, hedgerows, etc. Usually 4 – 6 eggs, incubated for 13 – 14 days, the young flying at 13 – 16 days.

Feeding: mainly seeds, berries, fruits, buds.

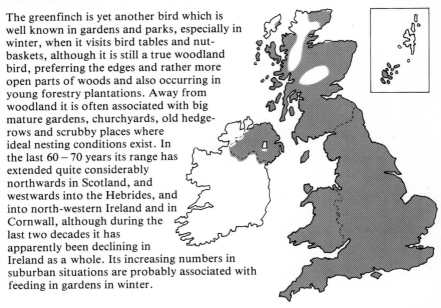

The greenfinch is yet another bird which is well known in gardens and parks, especially in winter, when it visits bird tables and nut-baskets, although it is still a true woodland bird, preferring the edges and rather more open parts of woods and also occurring in young forestry plantations. Away from woodland it is often associated with big mature gardens, churchyards, old hedge-rows and scrubby places where ideal nesting conditions exist. In the last 60 – 70 years its range has extended quite considerably northwards in Scotland, and westwards into the Hebrides, and into north-western Ireland and in Cornwall, although during the last two decades it has apparently been declining in Ireland as a whole. Its increasing numbers in suburban situations are probably associated with feeding in gardens in winter.

Siskin

Carduelis spinus

Size: 4¾ in (12 cm).

Recognition: very small finch; male mainly yellowish-green with black crown and chin, yellow rump, yellowish wingbar and sides of tail. Female greyer, much less yellow, no black on head.

Voice: main calls high 'tsi-zi' and a wheezing 'sooeet'. Song is rapid musical twittering, ending with long wheezing note.

Nesting: usually nests in conifers, often very high. Normally 3 – 5 eggs, incubated for about 11 – 12 days, young fledging at about 15 days.

Feeding: mainly seeds of trees.

♂

♀

The siskin is essentially a bird of coniferous woodland, though in winter it often appears in mixed woodland and, especially, alders. An interesting change in siskin behaviour has taken place in the last 15 years or so – they have started to come to peanuts in gardens in winter, which could well be partly responsible for their staying in and colonising new areas. Originally they were probably largely confined to the native Scottish pine forests, but since the 1850s they have spread into new areas, wherever conifers are present, and they have certainly benefited from the spread of forestry during the last 30 years. Breeding birds are now established in widely scattered localities in England and Wales, while in Ireland the siskin has been present for a long time following the large-scale planting of pines.

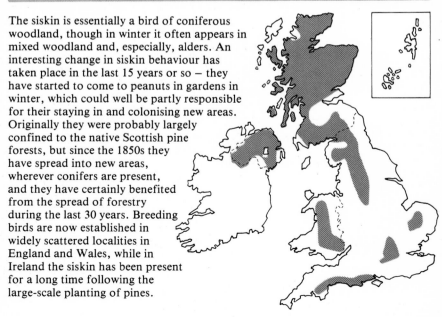

Redpoll

Acanthis flammea

Size: 5 in (13 cm).

Recognition: a small finch, brown above, streaked darker, and lighter below with streaked flanks. Crimson forehead, small black chin-patch.

Voice: high-pitched flight-call 'chuch-uch-uch-uch' is very distinctive; also 'teeoo, teeoo' and a plaintive 'sooeet'. Trilling, varied song, often in flight.

Nesting: varied nest-sites. Usually 4 – 5 eggs, incubated for about 10 – 11 days, the young flying at 11 – 14 days.

Feeding: mainly seeds, some insects and larvae.

Juv

Adult

Although redpolls may occur in almost any kind of woodland, they are perhaps most closely associated with birchwoods, alder woods, mixed carr, scrubby areas, heathland with scattered birches and, importantly, new forestry plantations. The widespread and large-scale increase in commercial forestry in the last 30 years since the war has undoubtedly played a large part in the dramatic increase in redpoll numbers. Many parts of the extreme north and west have only been colonised in the last dozen years or so. As the expansion continues, redpolls have even become hedgerow birds in some areas, and garden birds elsewhere. All this has taken place following a large decrease during the 1920s which in turn followed a marked increase and spread in the early years of this century.

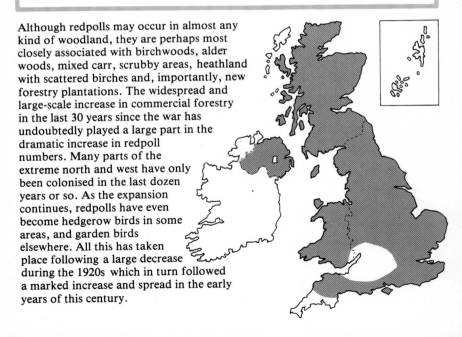

Bullfinch

Pyrrhula pyrrhula

Size: 5¾ in (14.5 cm).

Recognition: fairly stout finch, black cap, wings and tail and conspicuous white rump. Male rose-red below, blue-grey above, female browner grey above, pale pinkish-brown below.

Voice: usual call a soft, piping 'wheep'.

Nesting: normally nests low in trees, in evergreens, bushes, hedges, etc. Usually 4 – 5 eggs, incubated for 12 – 14 days, the young flying at 12-16 days.

Feeding: a variety of seeds, berries, fruits, often buds of shrubs and fruit trees in spring.

Bullfinches are mainly birds of the edges of woodland and scrubby areas which have also spread into old hedgerows, gardens, orchards and even new forestry plantations. In fruit-growing areas they are often regarded as pests and indeed can do considerable damage to commercial crops of apples, pears, cherries, plums and so on. In addition they eat many flower buds, especially later in winter when supplies of seeds and fruits are running low. Today, the species is widespread throughout most of Britain and Ireland, wherever suitable habitat exists, and is only absent from the extreme north and north-west and the westernmost parts of Ireland. It has probably expanded northwards and westwards during the last two centuries or so and numbers have apparently increased during the last 25 years.

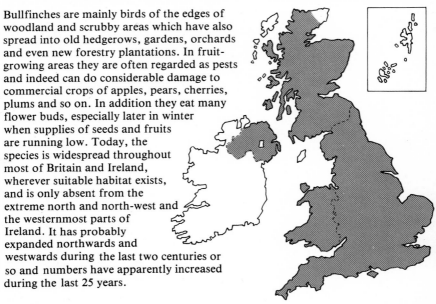

Crossbill

Loxia curvirostra

Adult

Juv

Size: 6½ in (16.5 cm).

Recognition: big-headed, short-tailed finch with the tips of the mandibles crossed. Fully adult male striking brick-red, younger males more orange, browner above; female greenish, with yellow on rump and underparts.

Voice: a loud, emphatic 'chip-chip-chip'. Song varied, trills, warbles, 'chip' calls etc.

Nesting: normally nests fairly high in pines. Usually 4 eggs, incubated for about 12 – 13 days, young flying at 17 – 25 days.

Feeding: mainly pine and spruce seeds.

Crossbills are conspicuously noisy and often very tame birds, feeding acrobatically on pine cones and often coming regularly to puddles, pools, etc. to drink. Their distribution is complicated, since it is mainly related to the productivity of the conifers which are the main source of food, as well as to the distribution of coniferous woodland itself; in addition, large influxes from Europe occur fairly often following 'good years', with crossbills staying after these big invasions to colonise new areas — e.g., the brecks in Norfolk and Suffolk after 1910 and the New Forest around the same time. The pine-feeding population in Highland Scotland occurs mainly in the old native pine forest; these birds have larger bills than the crossbills found elsewhere and are now regarded as a separate species — the Scottish crossbill.

Chaffinch

Fringilla coelebs

Size: 6 in (15 cm).

Recognition: conspicuous double white wingbars, white outer tail-feathers. Male has blue-grey crown and nape, chestnut mantle, greenish rump, pinkish underparts; female drabber.

Voice: loud 'pink, pink', a thin 'wheet' and a short 'chwit', rattling song ending with a flourish.

Nesting: normally nests in small trees or bushes. Usually 4 – 5 eggs, incubated for about 11 – 13 days, the young flying at about 13 – 14 days.

Feeding: mainly a wide variety of seeds, plus some fruits.

The chaffinch is the commonest and best-known finch, occurring almost anywhere where there are trees or bushes, and found in areas of scrub, parks and gardens. It is commonest, however, in mature broadleaved woodland. After the breeding season it is often highly gregarious, forming large mixed flocks with other finches and sparrows, often on farmland or in other open country. There may be as many as 7 million breeding pairs in Britain and Ireland, and certainly it is widely distributed, being absent as a nesting species only from the Outer Hebrides and the northern isles. Its distribution in Britain and Ireland has probably altered little this century, although there have been some fluctuations in the total population and it has also colonised a few new areas in the extreme north and north-west.

Tree Sparrow

Passer montanus

Size: 5½ in (14 cm).

Recognition: closely resembles house sparrow, but has smaller chocolate-brown crown, whitish cheeks and half-collar, small black cheek-spot, much smaller black bib.

Voice: short 'chik', 'chup', or a double 'chik-chup', rapid twittering and a very characteristic 'tek-tek' in flight.

Nesting: nests in holes in trees, cliffs, buildings, etc. Usually 4 – 6 eggs, incubated for about 12 – 14 days, young flying at 12 – 14 days.

Feeding: mainly seeds of various kinds; some insects.

Although they do occur close to human habitation in some areas, tree sparrows are much more 'countryside' birds than the more familiar house sparrow. They are found in a wide range of habitats, but are often closely associated with mature woodland or areas with old, scattered trees. They are often colonial nesters. Puzzling fluctuations in the sizes and fortunes of colonies are well known: there is a somewhat complicated pattern of presence, disappearance and recolonisation in Ireland, and many parts of Scotland, Wales and western England over the last 100 years or more. Since the early 1960s, however, tree sparrows have returned to Ireland and have regained ground in parts of Scotland, even colonising wholly new areas. Similarly, a gradual spread westwards has been discernible in Wales and southern England.

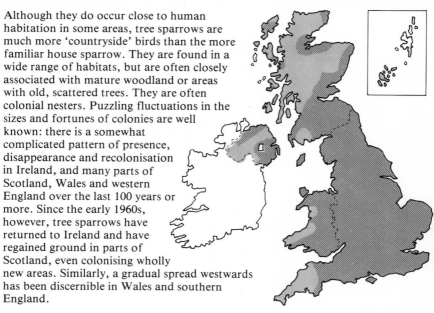

Woodlands and the Future

In this book, we have looked briefly at the chequered history of our woodlands, and have considered just one aspect of their extremely varied wildlife, woodland birds. What we have seen is a long history of the exploitation of woodland by man, on such a vast scale that the greater part of our tree cover has vanished. Some efforts at replanting and restoration have occurred, but only on a relatively small scale, with most of the present effort directed towards producing purely commercial forests. Demands on the land for more industry, more housing and roads and more intensive agriculture are, if anything, increasing: we cannot escape the fact that the remnants of our woodland are still under threat—not just woodlands, but the whole mosaic of little copses, thickets, belts of trees and individual trees which, in total, are of considerable importance. It is quite evident from our survey of woodland birds that no individual species is threatened with anything as dire as extinction, except on a purely local scale, and that a number of species are adaptable enough to cope with change, while others may even benefit (at least in the short term) from activities such as commercial forestry. Nevertheless, the loss of so much habitat means a gradual diminution in the total numbers of many woodland species and this in itself is cause enough for concern.

Basically, there is a need to preserve as much of our existing woodland as possible. Fortunately, there are signs that the tide is turning—local and national authorities concerned with planning are at last beginning to heed the advice of conservationists and to think in terms of preserving woods and trees wherever possible; even a few large industrial concerns are now interested in retaining as much of the 'natural' landscape around their centres of operations as is compatible with their other activities. But a great deal remains to be done. The basic idea that multi-purpose land-use is not only desirable but economically possible has been very, very slow to catch on. We still have a long way to go. Some of the biggest and best remnants of our forests are preserved in various ways by all sorts of organisations, not all of them wildlife conservation bodies, and sometimes we have otherwise unsavoury kings or politicians of the distant past to thank for that. Despite the continuing fragmentation of large estates throughout the British Isles, many private landowners are doing much to preserve their woodlands. Right across the board there is also a lot of evidence of new planting—a good sign, even if we could really do with a lot more attention to replanting native species and a lot less to turning to exotic, alien trees, often only because they 'look nice'.

Public and private conservation bodies have done much during the last 30 years to establish nature reserves where woodlands of national, regional or local importance can be preserved. What is even more important is that they have also identified, to a great extent, all those other sites which ought to be preserved: despite often chronic shortages of money, especially in the public sector, they are all persevering to buy, lease or manage by agreement still more reserves and considerable progress is being made towards encouraging others to preserve woodland through a slow but steady process of education and propaganda. In this direction, too, the positive achievements of the Farming and Wildlife Advisory Group must be mentioned. The Group demonstrates only too clearly that with goodwill and common sense even the apparently divergent aims of farmers and wildlife conservationists can be reconciled, to the benefit of both agriculture and wildlife. The Nature Conservancy Council, the statutory body responsible for nature conservation, has established a fine representative network of woodland National Nature Reserves in Great Britain (the map on page 157 shows the impressive spread of all their reserves, woodland and others, established so far). The Royal Society for the Protection of Birds has a number of woodland bird reserves of both national and regional importance, and plans to acquire more as funds permit. And at regional and county level, the many county naturalists' trusts we are so fortunate to possess in this country are, in effect, 'filling in' with the establishment of an impressive number of generally smaller reserves.

Woodland conservation does not stop at the mere acquisition of reserves: land needs to be managed effectively. On many fronts, naturalists and conservationists have carried out (and are still pursuing) research programmes which not only tell us which organisms are present and in what quantities but also what their requirements are and how these can best be met by intelligent, long-term management. In woodlands, this involves, for example, basic recording (much of it by amateurs) through such schemes as the Common Bird Census of the British Trust for Ornithology (B.T.O.), and many 'atlas' schemes, either at county or national level. The botanical atlas produced by the Botanical Society of the British Isles is a classic of its kind; it was the inspiration for many subsequent national mapping projects, including the splendid atlas of breeding bird distribution produced jointly by the

B.T.O. and the Irish Wildbird Conservancy. Such comprehensive and valuable works have, in their turn, encouraged 'atlasing' in many other countries.

As well as gathering facts, the conservation bodies are gaining experience and expertise in the actual processes of woodland managment with wildlife in mind—planting, weeding, the retention of dead timber as part of a natural ecosystem—and many other allied matters. The ancient art of coppicing, so essential to the proper management of some woodlands, and of growing and cropping osiers (a type of willow) have been revived by conservationists. By degrees, while this bank of knowledge and experience is being built up, increasingly large numbers of working volunteers are becoming involved in practical conservation, either through the national or local conservation bodies they can join, or through specialist 'agencies' like the British Trust for Conservation Volunteers. The growing involvement of young people in all these things is particularly encouraging. There is hope, then, with so many things going on, but, as was said earlier in another context, we still have a very long way to go.

On the face of it, considerable achievements have been made through the efforts of the Forestry Commission and their opposite numbers in Northern Ireland and Eire, and to a lesser extent private forestry operators, to increase the acreage of woodland or forest in these islands. In Great Britain, a slow increase in area is discernible: we now have about 9 per cent of our land under woodland or forest—which may seem a lot, but is really quite low when compared with, for example, 25 per cent in France and 29 per cent in West Germany. The claim is often made that forestry is beneficial to wildlife, along with statements to the effect that it enhances scenery and also puts to good use unused or under-used land (moors, hillsides, etc.). The fact that the main object of afforestation is to grow as much commercial timber as possible is never denied, but it is sometimes obscured by these other considerations. The scenic question is highly emotive and obviously subjective—but it is debatable whether a great sea of dense, monocultured conifers of alien species is always better than an open hillside, however, man-made the latter might also be, and I for one would take a lot of convincing that a big plantation was aesthetically more pleasing than a hanging oakwood in upland Wales, or a birch or pine wood in the Highlands.

The more burning questions are those concerning wildlife and land-use. As we have seen, young plantations, whether wholly new or replacing clear-felled timber, are of considerable value to a lot of birds—and, it follows, to an assortment of plants and insects; a few rare or uncommon birds have definitely benefited from afforestation, notably the hen harrier. But as plantations mature their value lessens in a number of ways: the alien spruces and pines are so dense in their closed ranks that little ground cover exists away from rides and firebanks and, while some birds and animals continue to use them and benefit from them, their species richness declines markedly. Dead wood is removed and, devoid of other plants and tree species, the aliens support far fewer insects than a native woodland. In many ways, commercial forestry would be far better for native wildlife were it more scattered, in smaller-sized and more open blocks, and more varied, and if this use of the land was better integrated with wildlife interests already there, but, alas, most of these ideas will always be attacked on economic grounds. The argument that commercial Scots pine is 'good' because this is a native tree is only partially true—nor does that other extraordinary twist of reasoning which suggests that a Norway or Sitka spruce plantation would be excellent if populated by introduced northern European or North American species stand up to close examination: there is simply no comparison between a spruce plantation and a real, natural spruce forest.

The other big problem over forestry, especially in upland Britain, is its potential impact on other valuable wildlife habitats. It is not difficult to make out a good case for forestry being economically more realistic than some of the highly-subsidised and unproductive forms of land-use currently practised on some of the higher ground in Wales and Scotland; some naturalists might even concede that trees, even conifer plantations, are better than sheep! And if agricultural techniques, improve sufficiently over the next half century to make better farming possible on marginal land, it could be just as harmful as forestry. What is at risk is a whole series of upland habitats which contain valuable (and in some cases quite rare) plant, animal and bird communities: on the bird side, the breeding grounds of some wading birds and birds of prey (notably merlins) and the large open areas required for hunting by some birds of prey (especially golden eagles and kites, but also hen harriers—despite the initial advantage they gain from new plantings) could well disappear. In the case of the eagle, we have an international responsibility since Scotland holds perhaps 20 per cent of the entire European population. Native woodland, too, is very much at risk: its replacement by commercial forestry, in either those upland areas where it still exists or in lowland areas, is most undesirable.

To date, too few constraints have been imposed on foresters as to where they should or should not plant, despite the genuine desire of some of them to integrate their plans with the needs of wildlife, and despite the efforts of forestry interests to carry out some wildlife conservation measures of their own and to develop public access and interest on the lands they hold. More progress must be made towards better balanced, long-term programme of afforestation both through better and more binding constraints where areas of value to wildlife are concerned and through much more all-round consultation with conservationists.

Even this very brief chapter indicates the need for more and better conservation. This means more and more public support and participation if it is to succeed. You can find out more, and do something positive to help, by joining one of the voluntary conservation organisations. The Royal Society for the Protection of Birds is the national conservation body on the ornithological side: full details of its activities and membership are available from: The Lodge, Sandy, Bedfordshire SG19 2DL. Any of the county naturalists' trusts (and in Scotland the Scottish Wildlife Trust) are well worth joining: you can find their addresses in the telephone directory (under the name of the county), or by writing for more information to their parent body, the Society for the Promotion of Nature Conservation at: The Green, Nettleham, Lincoln LN2 2NR. Those who are eager to roll up their sleeves and get cracking should lose no time in getting in touch with the British Trust for Conservation Volunteers at: c/o Zoological Society of London, Regents Park, London NW1 4RY. On the ornithological front, you should seriously consider joining the British Trust for Ornithology (Beech Grove, Tring, Hertfordshire) or the Irish Wildbird Conservancy (c/o The Royal Irish Academy, 19 Dawson Street, Dublin 2).

Glossary

Arboreal: tree-living.
Broadleaved: denotes shape of leaves; this is the opposite to the 'needle' type of leaf on conifers.
Calcareous: containing lime or limestone.
Call-note: any call made by a bird, as opposed to *song*.
Carr: wet, marshy or boggy copse with trees and shrubs.
Climax: highest development possible in the plant sucession for a plant community.
Conifer: type of tree which bears cones in which the seed is contained; pines, firs, etc.
Deciduous: type of tree or shrub which sheds its leaves in winter.
Drey: squirrel's nest.
Field-marks: particular, often diagnostic features of bird's plumage, useful in identification.
Fledging: able to fly (young birds).
Flight call: as 'call-note' above, but made when bird is flying.
Myxomatosis: virulent, tumour-forming disease of rabbits. This disease was purposely encouraged in Britain in 1954 to drastically reduce the rabbit population which were considered pests—with much damage to interdependent species including birds.

Pedunculate oak: with leaves on stalks.
Raptor: bird of prey.
Relict: left-over, remnant; an adjective as opposed to the noun 'relic'.
'Roding': display flight peculiar to the woodcock when searching for a mate.
Rufous: reddish-brown.
Sessile oak: with leaves without stalks.
Song-flight: special flight during which birds delivers song.
Tree-line: limit of growth, set by either altitude or latitude.
'Vermin era': period, which to some extent continues today, when gamekeepers and sportsmen killed birds that interfered with gamebirds, notably birds of prey such as the goshawk, honey buzzard and red kite, and owls.
Vinous: wine-coloured.

National Nature Reserves

The Nature Conservancy Council has established 159 National Nature Reserves; some are owned or leased by the Council, others are established under a nature reserve agreement with the owners. Information on any of these or about the Council itself can be obtained from its Great Britain Headquarters: Nature Conservancy Council, 20 Belgrave Square, London SW1X 8PY. N.B: All the reserves have different regulations and many require permits before entry. Get in touch with the regional offices before trying to enter them.

The following is a listing of all the 159 Reserves, region by region, with the address of the regional office of the Council, and the names of the Reserves followed by the number which keys it to the map.

England: South-west Region
Roughmoor, Bishops Hull, Taunton, Somerset TA1 5AA.
Arne (134); Avon Gorge (115); Axmouth-Lyme Regis Undercliffs (141); Bovey Valley Woodlands (137); Braunton Burrows (129); Bridgwater Bay (125); Dendles Wood (139); Ebbor Gorge (124); Hartland Moor (140); Morden Bog (133); Rodney Stoke (123); Shapwick Heath (126); Studland Heath (135); Yarner Wood (138).

England: South-east Region
'Zealds', Church Street, Wye, Ashford, Kent TN25 5BW.
Castle Hill (142); Ham Street Woods (128); Blean Woods (121); High Halstow (118); Kingley Vale (131); Lullington Heath (132); Stodmarsh (122); The Swale (143); Swanscombe Skull Site (119); Tring Reservoirs (104); Wye and Crundale Downs (127).

England: West Midland Region
Attingham Park, Shrewsbury, Salop SY4 4TW.
Chaddesley Woods (92); Chartley Moss (76); Derbyshire Dales (61); Rostherne Mere (56); Workman's Wood (144); Wren's Nest (85); Wybunbury Moss (65); Wyre Forest (145).

England: East Midland Region
P.O. Box 6, Godwin House, George Street, Huntingdon, Cambs PE18 6BU.

Castor Hanglands (83); Chippenham Fen (93); Holme Fen (86); Knocking Hoe (105); Monks Wood (89); Saltfleetby-Theddlethorpe Dunes (55); Woodwalton Fen (90).

England: East Anglia Region
60 Bracondale, Norwich, Norfolk NOR 58B.
Bure Marshes (81); Cavenham Heath (94); Hales Wood (106); Hickling Broad (80); Holkham (67); Leigh (117); Orfordness-Havergate (107); Scolt Head Island (66); Swanton Novers Woods (72); Thetford Heath (91); Walberswick (95); Weeting Heath (87); Westleton Heath (96); Winterton Dunes (77).

England: North-west Region
Blackwell, Bowness-on-Windermere, Windermere, Cumbria LA23 3JR.
Ainsdale Sand Dunes (54); Asbyscar (146); Blelham Bog (48); Clawthorpe Fell (147); Gait Burrows (148); Glasson Moss (45); Moor House (46); North Fen (49); Roudsea Wood (51); Rusland Moss (50).

England: North-east Region
33 Eskdale Terrace, Newcastle-upon-Tyne NE2 4DN.
Coom Rigg Moss (42); Lindisfarne (38); Long Gill (52); Upper Teesdale (47).

Scotland: South-west Region
The Castle, Loch Lomond Park, Balloch. Dunbartonshire.
Ben Lui (31); Caerlaverock (44); Cairnsmore of Fleet (149); Glasdrum Wood (29); Glen Diomhan (37); Kirkconnell Flow (43); Loch Lomond (36); Silver Flowe (41); Taynish (150); Tynron Juniper Wood (40).

Scotland: South-east Region
12 Hope Terrace, Edinburgh EH9 2AS.
Ben Lawers (151); Caenlochan (25); Isle of May (35); Loch Leven (34); Meall Nan Tarmachan (30); Morton Lochs (33); Rannoch Moor (28); Tentsmuir Point (32); Whitlaw Mosses (39).

Scotland: North-west Region
Fraser Darling House, 9 Culduthel Road, Inverness IV2 2 AG.
Allt Nan Carnan (17); Ariundle Oakwood (152); Beinn Eighe (16); Coile Thocabhaig (153); Corrieshalloch (13); Glen Roy (24); Gualin (7); Inchnadamph (9); Invernaver (6);

Inverpolly (10); Loch Druidibeg (18); Loch Maree Islands (159); Monach Isles (14); Mound Alderwoods (12); Nigg and Udale Bays (158); North Rona and Sula Sgeir (3,4); Rassal Ashwood (15); Rhum (21); St Kilda (11); Strathy Bog (8); Strathfarrar (153).

Scotland: North-east Region

Wyne-Edwards House, 17 Rubislaw Terrace, Aberdeen AB1 1XE.

Cairngorms (22); Craigellachie (20); Dinnet Oakwood (23); Haaf Fruney (2); Hermaness (1); Keen of Hamar (154). Morrone Birkwoods (26); Muir of Dinnet (155); Noss (5); St Cyrus (27); Sands of Forvie (19).

Wales: North Wales Region

Penrhos Ffordd, Bangor, Gwynedd LL57 2LQ.

Cader Idris (82); Coed Aber (156); Coed Camlyn (71); Coed Cymerau (69); Coed Dolgarrog (60); Coed Ganllwyd (79); Coed Gorswen (59); Coed Y Rhygen (74); Coed Tremadoc (70); Coedydd Maentwrog (68); Cors Erddreiniog (57); Cwm Glas Crafnant (63); Cwm Idwal (62); Morfa Dyffryn (78); Morfa Harlech (73); Newborough Warren/Ynys Llanddwyn (58); Rhiong (75); Y Wyddfa-Snowdon (64).

Wales: Dyfed-Powys Region

Plas Gogerddan, Aberystwyth, Dyfed SY23 3 EB.

Allt Rhyd y Groes (99); Coed Rheidol (88); Cors Tregaron (97); Craig Cerrig Gleisiad (100); Craig y Cilau (101); Dyfi (84); Nant Irfon (98); Ogof Ffynnon Ddu (157); Skomer (111).

Wales: South Wales Region

44 The Parade, Roath, Cardiff CF2 3AB.

Cwm Clydach (102); Gower Coast (113); Oxwich (114); Whiteford (112).

National Nature Reserves

158

Index